PRAISE FOR

OPTION STRATEGIES FOR DIRECTIONLESS MARKETS

Trading with Butterflies, Iron Butterflies, and Condors

by Anthony J. Saliba
with Joseph C. Corona and Karen E. Johnson

"*Option Strategies for Directionless Markets* offers a practical approach to trading butterfly strategies. I found it very comprehensive. The what-if scenarios were especially helpful."

—MATT BROWN
Sales Trader, Piper Jaffray

"With detailed and insightful discussions on strategy application and position management, this book offers a tactical approach—something I have not found in other books."

—GÖRAN EKMAN
Head of Sales, Financial Training, OMX

"Change is constant—new and improved technology every day and market change continual. To keep up and gain an edge, the trading strategies and how-to approach detailed in Tony Saliba's *Option Strategies for Directionless Markets* can take you to the next level of options professionalism."

—KEN HEATH
Publisher, *Traders Magazine*

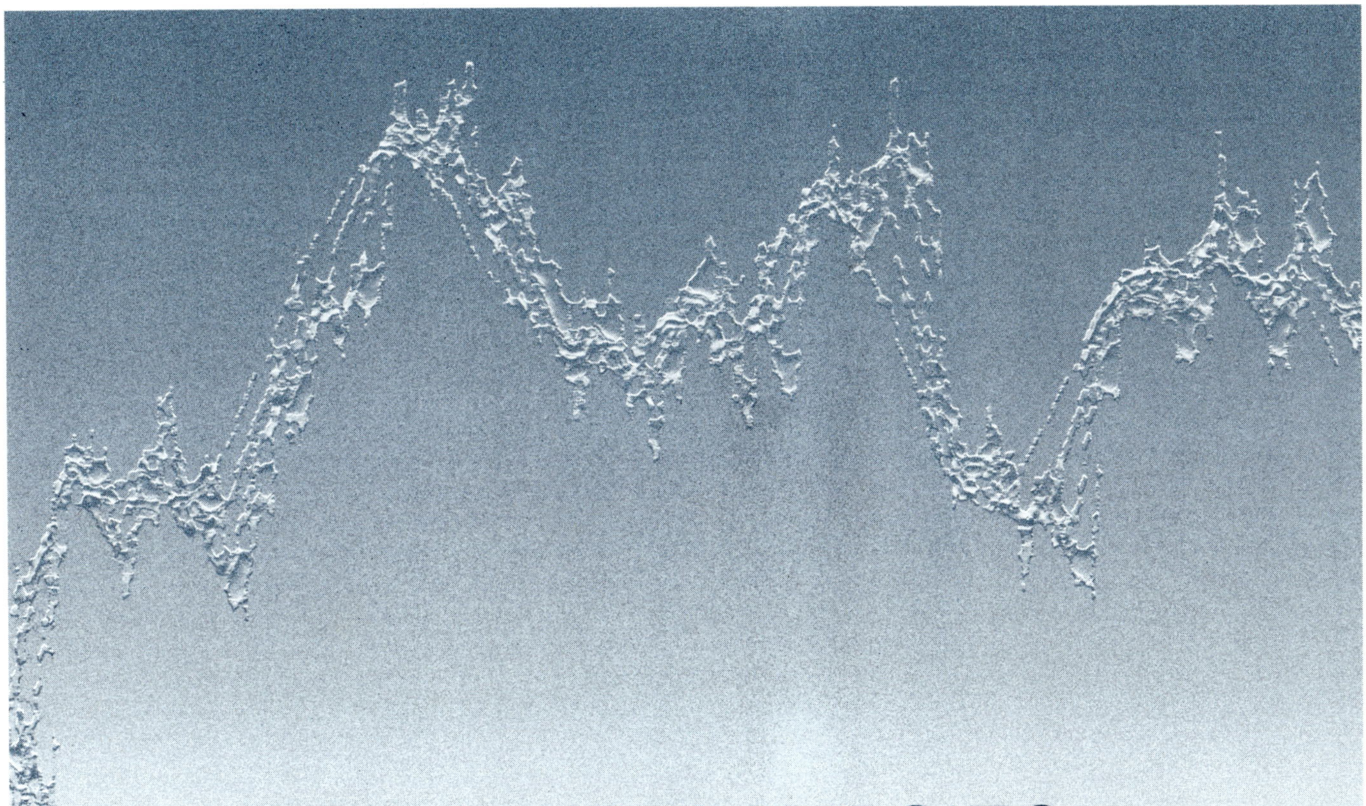

OPTION STRATEGIES FOR DIRECTIONLESS MARKETS

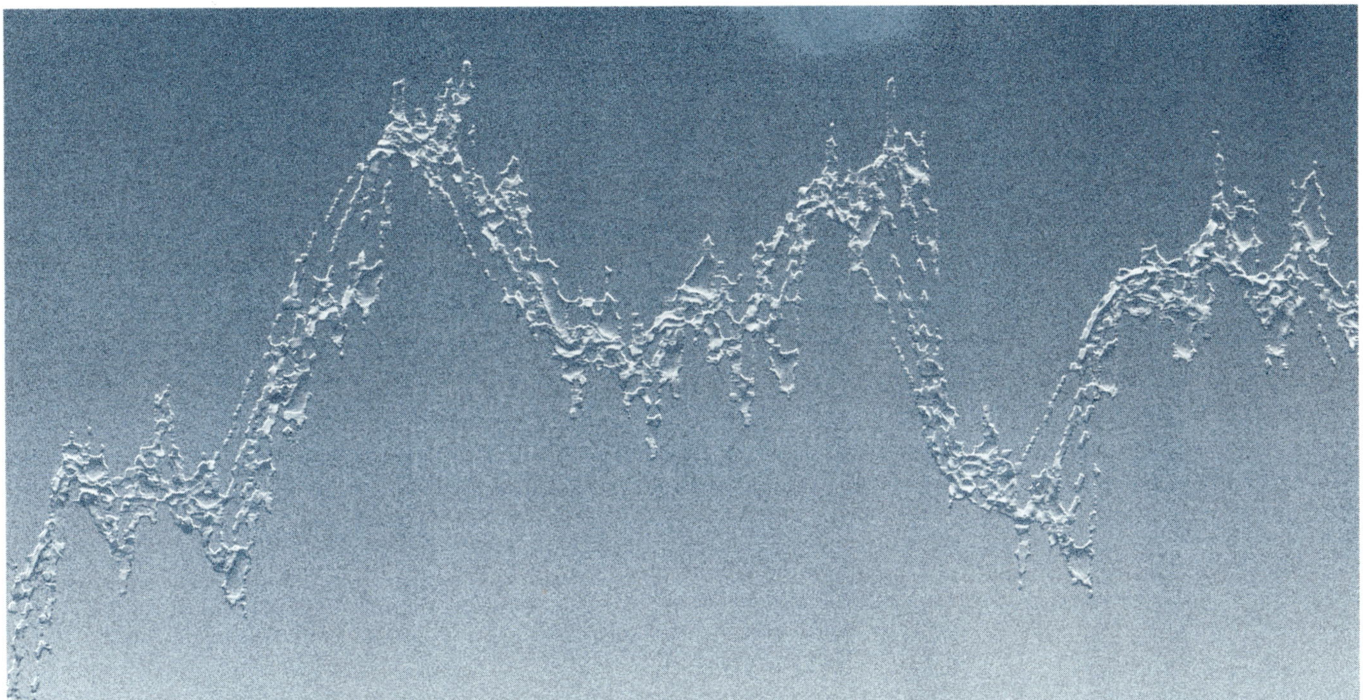

OPTION STRATEGIES FOR DIRECTIONLESS MARKETS

Trading with Butterflies, Iron Butterflies, and Condors

ANTHONY J.
SALIBA

with Joseph C. Corona
and Karen E. Johnson

Viva Books

New Delhi | Mumbai | Chennai | Kolkata | Bangalore | Hyderabad | Kochi | Guwahati

First Indian Edition 2010

VIVA BOOKS PRIVATE LIMITED

- 4737/23 Ansari Road, Daryaganj, New Delhi 110 002
  E-mail: vivadelhi@vivagroupindia.net, Tel. 42242200
- 76, Service Industries, Shirvane, Sector 1, Nerul, Navi Mumbai 400 706
  E-mail: vivamumbai@vivagroupindia.net, Tel. 27721273, 27721274
- Jamals Fazal Chambers, 26 Greams Road, Chennai 600 006
  E-mail: vivachennai@vivagroupindia.net, Tel. 28290304, 28294241
- B-103, Jindal Towers, 21/1A/3 Darga Road, Kolkata 700 017
  E-mail: vivakolkata@vivagroupindia.net, Tel. 22836381, 22816713
- 7, Sovereign Park Apartments, 56-58, K. R. Road, Basavanagudi, Bangalore 560 004
  E-mail: vivabangalore@vivagroupindia.net, Tel. 26607409, 26607410
- 101-102 Mughal Marc Apartments, 3-4-637 to 641, Narayanguda, Hyderabad 500 029
  E-mail: vivahyderabad@vivagroupindia.net, Tel. 27564481, 27564482
- Beevi Towers, First Floor, SRM Road, Kaloor, Kochi 682 018, Kerala
  E-mail: vivakochi@vivagroupindia.net, Tel: 0484-2403055, 2403056
- 232, GNB Road, Beside UCO Bank, Silpukhuri, Guwahati 781 003
  E-mail: vivaguwahati@vivagroupindia.net, Tel: 0361-2666386

www.vivagroupindia.com

Published by arrangement with

Bloomberg Press
731 Lexington Avenue
New York, NY 10022

This edition is for sale in the Indian subcontinent only. Not for export elsewhere.

ISBN : 978-81-309-1121-2

Published by Vinod Vasishtha for Viva Books Private Limited, 4737/23, Ansari Road, Daryaganj, New Delhi - 110 002.

Printed and bound by Raj Press, R-3, Inderpuri, New Delhi - 110 012.

Important Disclosures

Following are several important disclosures we are required to make according to the rules of the Chicago Board Options Exchange (CBOE), by which we are governed. We encourage you to read them.

- Prior to buying or selling an option, one must receive a copy of the booklet "Characteristics and Risks of Standardized Options." Copies of this document are available at www.theocc.com/publications/risks/riskchap1.jsp or from International Trading Institute, Ltd., 311 South Wacker, Suite 4700, Chicago, IL 60606.
- Options involve risk and are not suitable for all investors.
- In order to trade strategies discussed in this book, an individual must first have his account approved by a broker/dealer for that specific trading level.
- No statement in this book should be construed as a recommendation to purchase or sell a security or as an attempt to provide investment advice.
- Writers of uncovered calls or puts will be obligated to meet applicable margin requirements for certain option strategies discussed in this book.
- For transactions that involve buying and writing multiple options in combination, it may be impossible at times to simultaneously execute transactions in all of the options involved in the combination.
- There is increased risk exposure when you exercise or close out of one side of a combination while the other side of the trade remains outstanding.
- Because all option transactions have important tax considerations, you should consult a tax adviser as to how taxes will affect the outcome of contemplated options transactions.
- The examples in this book do not include commissions and other costs. Transaction costs may be significant, especially in option strategies calling for multiple purchases and sales of options, such as spreads and straddles.
- Most spread transactions must be done in a margin account.

Contents

List of Figures

Acknowledgments

I would like to thank the many individuals who helped make the writing of this book possible.

First I would like to thank my coauthors, Joe Corona and Karen Johnson. Realizing the need for an educational tool focusing on strategies that can be used to take advantage of a sideways market, Karen came up with the idea to write a book about the butterfly strategy and its affiliates. Joe Corona brought his trading expertise and writing skills to the table. The book would not have been possible without their dedication to this project.

I would also like to thank David Schmueck, my firm's registered options principal. He went beyond the call of duty in helping us edit and proofread the book. His input was very helpful in making sure the book's content was appropriate for the intended audience.

Stephen Isaacs of Bloomberg Press was a champion in publishing this book, as was my agent Cynthia Zigmund.

Lastly I would like to thank Chris Hausman, Scott Mollner, Carolyn Corona, and Christine Fisher for their help in proofreading portions of the manuscript. Their insights and suggestions were invaluable.

Anthony J. Saliba
Founder
International Trading Institute

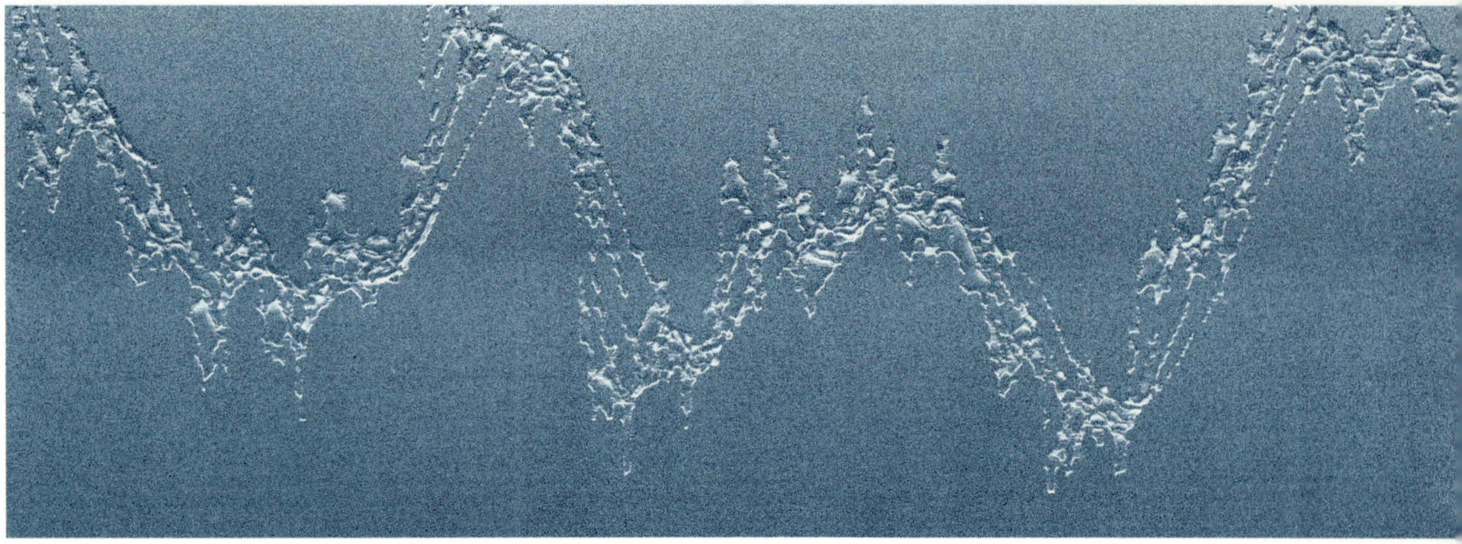

Introduction

For options traders, these are the best of times. A "perfect storm" of technology and competition has eroded the traditional advantages of access, information, and cost enjoyed by market makers and other professionals. These changes in the industry have helped open the door to the individual to participate in the options market in ways that would have been practically impossible just a few years ago.

Options can now be priced, executed, and managed electronically using many trading platforms, and these same technological advances have allowed brokers to reduce their commissions dramatically. Penny pricing and portfolio-based margining may serve only to further level the playing field.

Innovations at the exchange level allowing the electronic matching and processing of complex orders have stimulated greater participation and thus greater liquidity in these types of structures. Strategies that were previously "untouchable" by the individual investor may now be within reach, allowing the individual to express complex market views involving direction or lack thereof, timing, magnitude, velocity, and volatility levels.

In our first book, *The Options Workbook, 3rd Edition* (Dearborn Publishing, 2004), we introduced the entire options strategy toolbox. In this book, we explore strategies that address a directionless or sideways market: the butterfly and its variations, including the iron butterfly, condor, broken-wing butterfly, and pterodactyl.

We introduce the basics of long butterfly spreads and long condor spreads, including structure, P&L diagrams, and various scenarios. We also take a look at the Greeks (delta, gamma, theta, and vega) to see how they are used to measure the sensitivity of an option to changing conditions—a key factor in understanding long butterfly and condor spread structures. In later chapters, we explore using the butterfly structure as a trading vehicle for more aggressive trading tactics.

A detailed discussion on strategy application and position management is offered for each structure. Numerous charts and graphs help illustrate key concepts throughout each chapter.

It's one thing to read about these structures and strategies, but it's quite another to implement them in your own trading. So, at the end of each chapter you will find exercises and a quiz to test your understanding of the concepts presented. There is a final exam in the back of the book to further test your comprehension of the material covered.

You may also wish to check out our website, www.itichicago.com, for additional option strategy discussions.

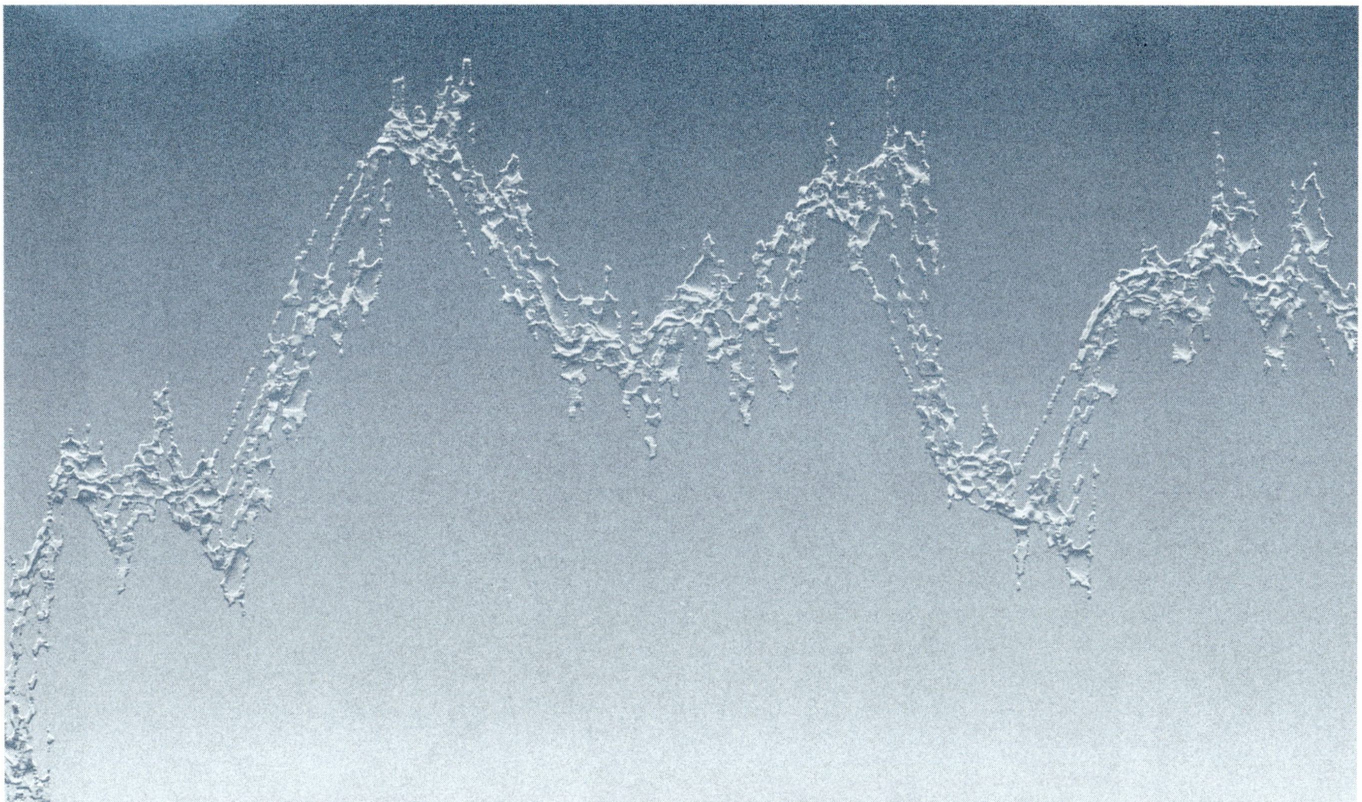

OPTION STRATEGIES FOR DIRECTIONLESS MARKETS

1

Strategies for the Directionless Market

Options continue to grow in popularity with investors. According to the Options Industry Council, volume in 2006 grew 34.8 percent over 2005, with more than two billion contracts traded. Investors are realizing that options can be profitable components of their portfolios and may offer some advantages over outright stock positions.

One of the many possible advantages of using options is the ability to build a custom strategy to fit a particular market view or situation. One does not need to be restricted to "bullish" or "bearish" in order to profitably participate in the marketplace. Market views encompassing direction (or lack thereof), magnitude, velocity, timing, and volatility all can be traded using option combinations or spreads that fit a specific market situation.

One of the most common market conditions that force the bulls and the bears to the bench is the "directionless" or "sideways" market. To a directional trader, a directionless market is a curse, where one continually gets whipsawed and forced out of the market as it bounces up and down but ultimately goes nowhere. However, to the option trader this situation can be quite profitable if the right strategy is applied.

WHAT IS A DIRECTIONLESS MARKET?

A directionless market occurs when the forces of supply (selling) and demand (buying) are not powerful enough to push prices into a directional trend. The market then begins to move sideways for a period of time. There is no "standard" length of time a market needs to go sideways to be deemed directionless; it is subjective and up to the observer. These sideways periods may form from a consolidation phase, where the market decides to take a "rest" after a directional move (see **Figure 1.1**), a waiting

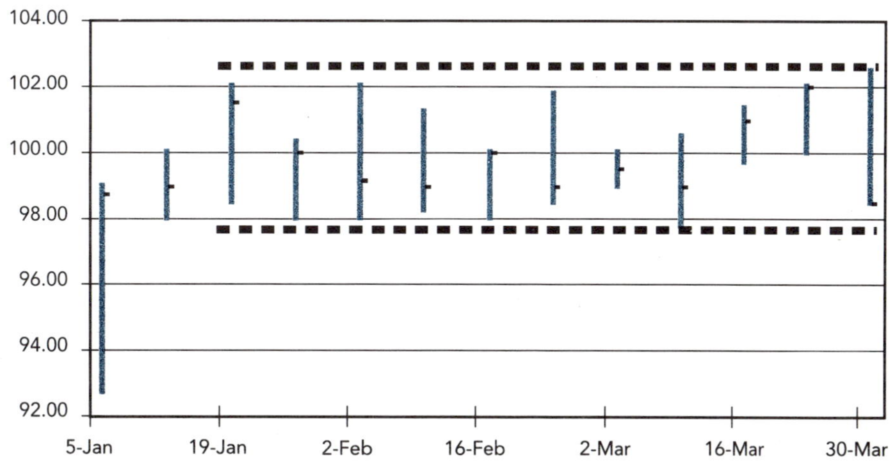

Figure 1.1 Consolidation *Source: Corona Derivatives, LLC*

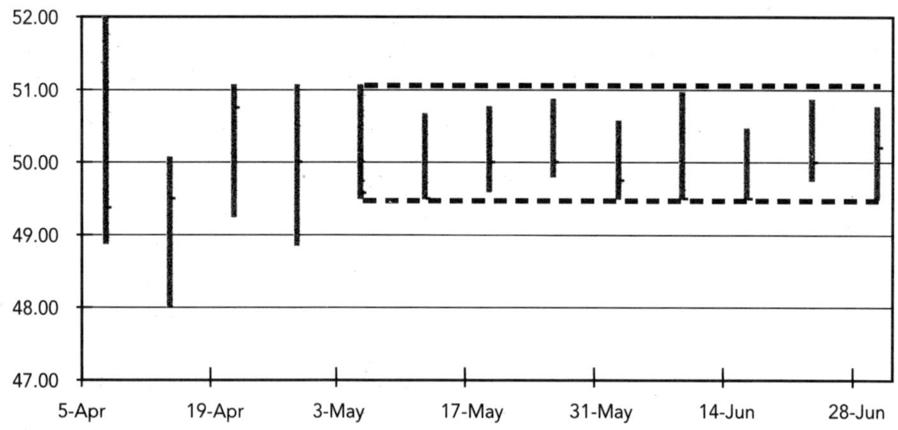

Figure 1.2 Seasonal Sideways *Source: Corona Derivatives, LLC*

period before important data are released, a prelude to a reversal of trend, or a seasonal condition where there is just not enough interest or activity to force the market into a particular direction (see **Figure 1.2**).

IDENTIFYING THE DIRECTIONLESS MARKET

Directionless markets are identified by observing price action. Technical analysis tools can be especially helpful in identifying an underlying directionless stock or index. Bar charts, candlestick charts, Market Profile, and other types of graphic representation of price action over time can be used. In addition, technical indicators, particularly "strength of trend" indicators, can be employed to help identify situations where trend strength is low and a directionless market is likely to persist. One doesn't have to be a technical wizard to spot a potentially directionless market. "Eyeballing" a price chart is usually sufficient, but there are a few basic concepts that should be understood.

Support and Resistance

Support and resistance levels represent price levels or zones where demand (buying pressure) or supply (selling pressure) materializes and halts falling prices or rising prices, respectively. Support and resistance levels can form within uptrends, downtrends, or directionless markets.

- **Support**

Support is a price level or zone located below the current market price where buyers become more willing to buy and sellers are reluctant to sell. The buyers overwhelm the sellers in or near these zones, forcing prices back up and preventing the price from falling below the support level. Support levels or zones are determined by connecting reaction lows or "valleys" of price action with a line. It takes at least two reaction lows near the same price to form a support level. The more reaction lows that occur in this

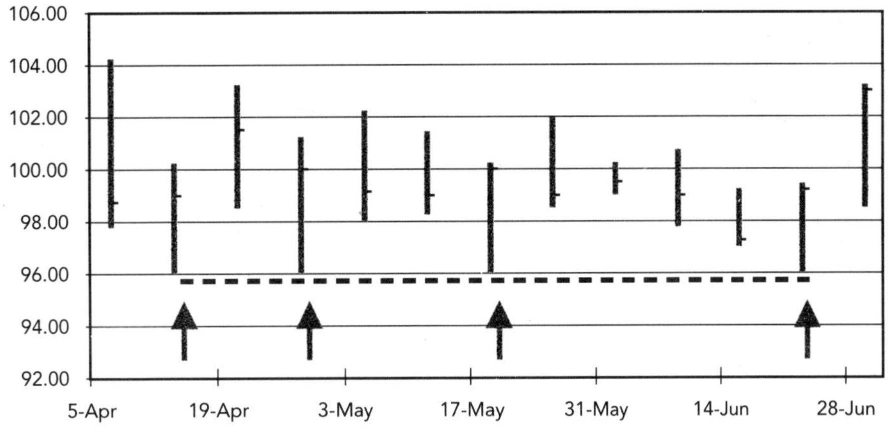

Figure 1.3 Support *Source: Corona Derivatives, LLC*

area the stronger the support level is seen to be. **Figure 1.3** illustrates this concept. The arrows identify the reaction lows which are then connected to form a support level.

- **Resistance**

Resistance is a price level or zone located above the current market price where sellers become more willing to sell and buyers are reluctant to buy. The sellers overwhelm the buyers in or near these zones, forcing prices back down and preventing the price from rising above resistance. Resistance levels or zones are determined by connecting reaction highs or "peaks" of price action with a line. It takes at least two reaction highs near the same price to form a resistance level. The more reaction highs that occur in this area, the stronger the resistance level is seen to be. **Figure 1.4** illustrates this concept. The arrows identify the reaction highs which are then connected to form a resistance level.

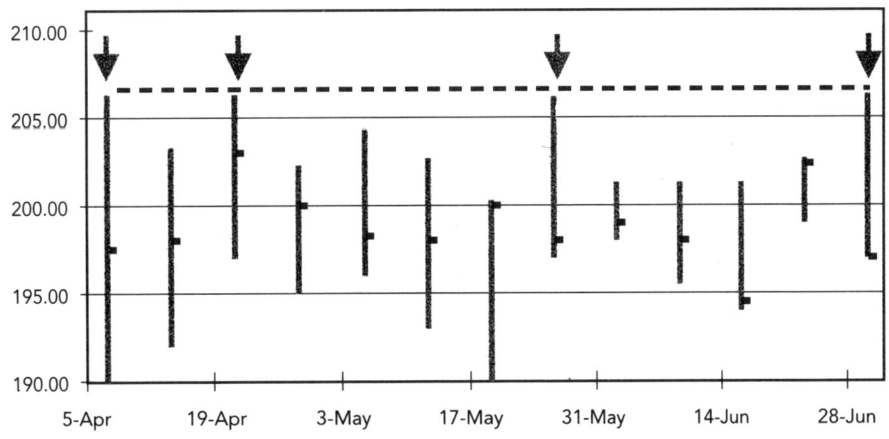

Figure 1.4 Resistance *Source: Corona Derivatives, LLC*

The Trading Range Market

When the forces of supply and demand equalize, a stalemate occurs and the market moves sideways between support and resistance levels within a trading range until one side can build up enough strength to finally overwhelm the other. Visualize two opposing armies entrenched directly across the battlefield from each other with neither having enough strength to break through the front line of the other. Attacks by each side on the other's front line are easily repulsed and neither side advances. The stalemate persists until one side finally builds up enough strength to break through the front line of the other. This is analogous to the classic directionless market (see **Figure 1.5** below).

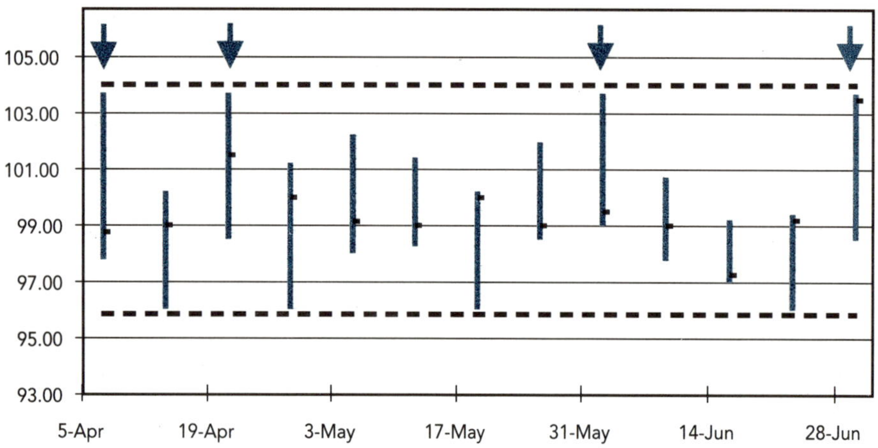

Figure 1.5 Trading Range *Source: Corona Derivatives, LLC*

The Trend Is Your Friend (Even When There Isn't One)

One of the oldest sayings in trading is "The trend is your friend." In other words, it is best to trade in the direction of the prevailing price trend because even if the trader's timing when entering a position is off a little bit, the underlying trend will eventually resume and come to the rescue. This, of course, doesn't always happen because trends typically end. Markets may trend longer and further than most would believe; therefore, trading with the prevailing price trend generally may be a good idea. This also may be true of the directionless market. Even though it is sometimes referred to as a "trendless" market, the directionless market does have a price trend—sideways—and it is important to consider this trend as well. Indicators that measure the strength of a trend (or lack of it) also can be helpful in identifying or confirming directionless trade possibilities.

Using Technical Indicators

There are almost as many technical indicators as there are stars in the sky—and certainly too many to attempt to cover here. However, a certain class of indicators, strength of trend indicators, can be used in conjunction with price charts to help identify markets that are directionless and have low trend strength (and, therefore, are likely to remain directionless).

Some of the better-known indicators include J. Welles Wilder's Average Directional Index (ADX) and Average True Range (ATR). Bollinger Bands and other volatility-based indicators also can be helpful in identifying low-volatility (directionless) situations. These and many other technical indicators can be found in most off-the-shelf technical analysis software packages. As with all technical indicators, it is important they be used with price charts for purposes of confirmation rather than on their own.

Important Factors

Regardless of what methods or tools are used to identify the directionless market, there are some important factors to consider when analyzing an underlying instrument for a possible directionless option strategy. Most important are the price levels involved. Support and resistance levels need to be identified, along with the point or area to where price tends to revert as it meanders up and down. These levels are of key importance for strike (exercise price) selection when constructing the strategy to be used. It also is important that the underlying instrument being analyzed appears likely to remain in the directionless mode for the period of time that corresponds to the time horizon the investor has chosen.

PROFITING FROM A DIRECTIONLESS MARKET

So what type of option strategies will theoretically profit from a directionless market? If a market is directionless and is hovering around the same prices every day or floundering inside a trading range, then the only thing really changing on a day-to-day basis is the passage of time. So it follows that those option strategies that are neutral in terms of direction and benefit from the passage of time (strategies with positive time decay) are the best for taking advantage of a directionless market.

Time Decay

The price of an option has two components: intrinsic value and extrinsic value. Intrinsic value is the amount by which an option is in-the-money. A call option is in-the-money if the price of the underlying is above the strike price. A put option is in-the-money if the price of the underlying is below the strike price. Any remaining value is extrinsic value. At-the-money options and out-of-the-money options are composed entirely of extrinsic value. The amount of extrinsic value in an option depends on many factors, including underlying price, interest rates, dividends, time until expiration, and implied volatility. The more uncertainty there is

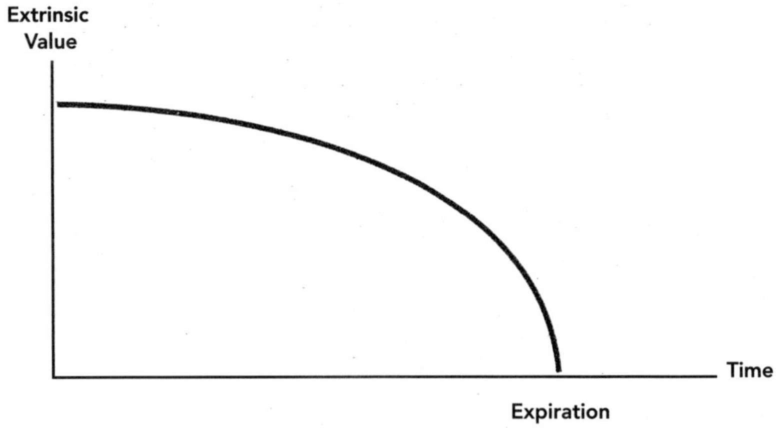

Figure 1.6 Time Decay *Source: Corona Derivatives, LLC*

about the option's possible value (for example, higher volatility, greater time to expiration), the greater the extrinsic value of the option. Conversely, the more certainty there is about an option's value (for example, lower volatility, less time until expiration), the lower the extrinsic value of the option.

Theoretically, an option loses a portion of its extrinsic value every day, and, over time, an option will lose all of its extrinsic value. This is referred to as "time decay." Because of time decay, buyers of options theoretically lose money every day, while sellers of options theoretically gain money every day. Time decay is quantified by theta (see **Figure 1.6**).

Theta

Theta is defined as the sensitivity of an option's price to the passage of time. It is usually quantified as the loss in an option's extrinsic value over one day's time. Long options have negative theta, and short options have positive theta. Some other important characteristics of theta:

- Theta of at-the-money options is greatest
- Theta of at-the-money options rises sharply as expiry approaches
- Theta of in-the-money and out-of-the money options falls as expiry approaches

Looking at **Figure 1.7**, one can see that the theta of an option or option position is highly dependent on the location of the strike(s) relative to the underlying price—the "moneyness" of the option(s)—as well as time to expiration. It is important to identify the boundaries of the directionless market as well as the area of mean reversion, in order to structure the position so it will have the greatest theta in the area where the underlying is most likely to trade.

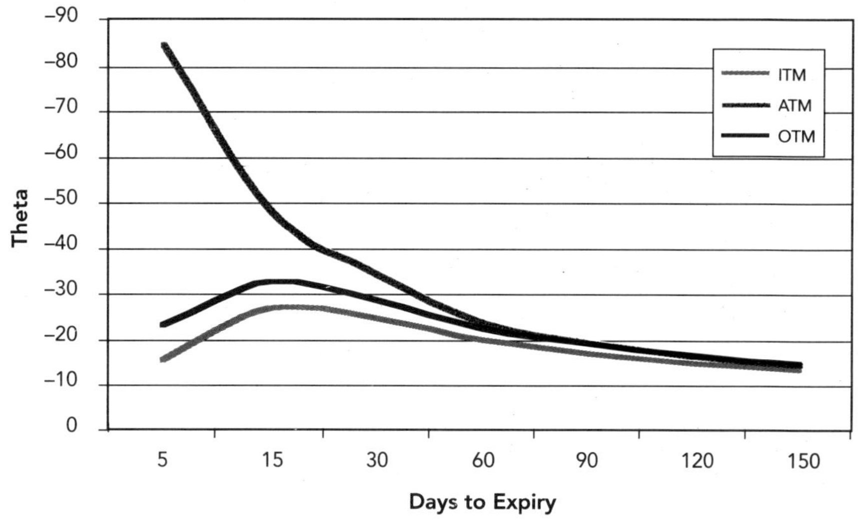

Figure 1.7 Theta Over Time *Source: Corona Derivatives, LLC*

OPTION STRATEGIES TO ADDRESS THE DIRECTIONLESS MARKET

An option strategy with positive time decay (positive theta) and a neutral directional bias theoretically will profit from a directionless market. As time passes and the underlying continues to move in a sideways motion, the options will lose some of their extrinsic value through time decay, making the position profitable. There are several different option strategies that fit this type scenario, some more aggressive than others. The long butterfly (and its variations) and the long at-the-money calendar spread are limited risk spreads, available for the individual investor. Calendar spreading can be a complicated endeavor that indeed merits a book of its own. In this book, we will focus on the simpler of the two strategies, the long butterfly.

Long Butterfly

The long butterfly is a unique option strategy that can be used to address the directionless market. A long butterfly is constructed using three (usually) adjacent strikes, purchasing the lower strike option, selling two options at the middle strike, and purchasing the higher strike option. The long butterfly has several variations and can be constructed using calls, puts, or a mixture of both. We explore the structure of these variations, including iron butterflies, condors, pterodactyls, and others, in later chapters.

Strike selection is very important when addressing the directionless market with a long butterfly. The middle strike should be located in the middle of the expected trading range. Placing the middle strike of the long butterfly at-the-money creates a position that does not have a directional bias and has a positive theta. Recall that at-the-money options have a higher theta than away-from-the-money options. Even though a long butterfly has an equal number of long and short options, locating the middle strike at-the-money gives the structure a positive theta.

The strength of the long butterfly is that it is a limited-risk strategy (see **Figure 1.8**). If the market suddenly breaks out of the trading range and is no longer directionless, the investor will likely experience a loss, but is not exposed to unlimited risk.

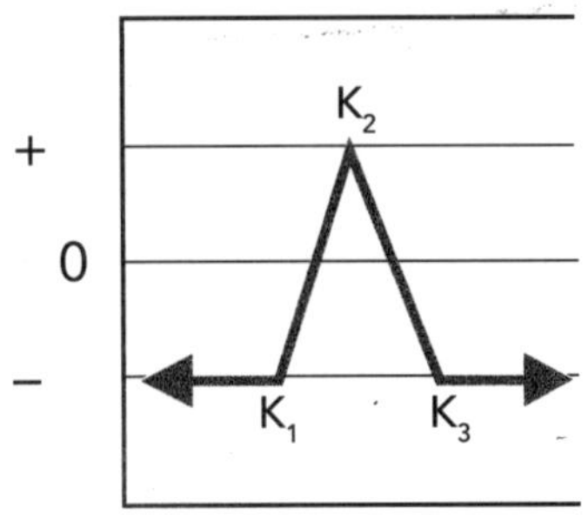

K = strike price; x-axis = the underlying price at expiration

Strategy:	Long 1 call at K_1; short (sell) 2 calls at K_2; long 1 call at K_3 (same expiration).
Direction basis:	Stable
Profit potential:	$(K_3 - K_1)/2$ – debit
Loss potential:	Debit (net premium paid)
Breakevens:	K_1 + debit; K_3 – debit

Figure 1.8 Long Butterfly Payout *Source: Corona Derivatives, LLC*

The long butterfly can also be a great trading vehicle, offering trading opportunity and some flexibility. There are several option strategies embedded in this strategy. There is a bull spread, a bear spread, a short straddle, and a long strangle—all contained in the long butterfly! These embedded structures allow the investor the additional flexibility to trade in and out of a long butterfly strategy in stages, depending on market view. Components can be added or subtracted as one's market view changes.

The following chapters are devoted exclusively to the use of the long butterfly and its many variations all of which attempt to take advantage of the directionless market.

SUMMARY

A "directionless market" is a condition in which the price of a stock or index is moving sideways over time. Although there are daily up and down fluctuations, no sustained progress is made either to the upside or to the downside. Such a market is sometimes referred to as "trendless," but in reality, the trend is sideways.

When a stock or index meanders in a directionless state, it usually will begin to form support and resistance levels, which tend to act as the boundaries of the directionless zone. Support and resistance levels may be detected by observing the price action or through technical analysis.

Options traders may take advantage of this type of market action by initiating positions with positive time decay and no directional bias. A position with positive time decay is a position that will theoretically increase in value every day through the erosion of the extrinsic value of the component options in the position.

There are several basic options strategies that have positive time decay and no directional bias, but with the exception of the long calendar spread, the long butterfly, long condor, and other long "winged" structures are the most flexible and most important, have limited risk, and therefore, are most appropriate for the individual investor.

2

Long Butterfly Spread Basics

CONCEPT REVIEW

Vertical spread. The simultaneous purchase and sale of options with the same class and expiration, but with different strike prices. Depending on which strike is bought and which strike is sold, it can have either a bullish or bearish bias. For example: XYZ July 100/105 call vertical spread. If the trader were bullish, he would buy the 100 call and sell the 105 call; if bearish, he would buy the 105 call and sell the 100 call.

Bear spread. A vertical spread with a bearish bias where one purchases a higher strike option and sells a lower strike option of the same class and expiration. A bear spread using calls (also known as a *short call spread*) will result in a credit, and a bear spread using puts (also known as a *long put spread*) will result in a debit.

Bull spread. A vertical spread with a bullish bias where one purchases a lower strike option and sells a higher strike option of the same class and expiration. A bull spread using calls (also known as a *long call spread*) will result in a debit, and a bull spread using puts (also known as a *short put spread*) will result in a credit.

Credit spread. A vertical spread where the option sold has a higher value than the option purchased, resulting in a net credit. A call bear spread and a put bull spread are examples of credit spreads.

Debit spread. A vertical spread where the option purchased has a higher value than the option sold, resulting in a net debit. A call bull spread and a put bear spread are examples of debit spreads.

As explained in Chapter 1, a long butterfly spread can be constructed using calls, puts, or combinations of both calls and puts. When both calls and puts are used, the strategy is referred to as an *iron butterfly*. Regardless of how it is constructed, if the effective price is the same, the profit and loss profile will be the same. We will discuss these issues at length when we explore iron butterflies and trading tactics. First, the basics.

THE CALL BUTTERFLY

Structure

A long call butterfly incorporates three strikes all having the same expiration cycle. It is constructed by purchasing a lower strike (K_1) call, selling two calls at a middle strike (K_2), and purchasing one higher strike (K_3) call. (See **Figure 2.1**). Typically the strikes selected are equidistant. If they are not, it is known as a *broken-wing butterfly*. We will discuss these and other variants in a later chapter.

Call	Strike	Put
+1	K_1	
−2	K_2	
+1	K_3	

Figure 2.1 Structure of the Long Call Butterfly Spread
Source: Corona Derivatives, LLC

The +1/−2/+1 structure is the signature of the long butterfly position. Regardless of whether it is a long call butterfly, long put butterfly, or long iron butterfly, it will always have this structure. The long options at the outside strikes are commonly referred to as the "wings," while the two short options at the middle strike are referred to as the "body," or "guts."

A quick inspection of Figure 2.1 reveals some interesting characteristics:

- The long call butterfly can be viewed as a combination of two vertical spreads; it is a bull spread (long call spread or *debit spread*, combining the lower two strikes) overlapped by a bear spread (short call spread or *credit spread*, combining the upper two strikes). (See **Figure 2.2**.)

Long Call Spread K_1,K_2	+	Short Call Spread K_2,K_3	=	Long Call Butterfly K_1,K_2,K_3	Strike
+1				+1	K_1
–1		–1		–2	K_2
		+1		+1	K_3

Figure 2.2 Long Call Butterfly Decomposition Diagram
Source: Corona Derivatives, LLC

- Because the trader is buying the vertical call spread (the lower two strikes) and selling the vertical call spread (the upper two strikes), he usually has to pay for a long call butterfly, since, with calls, the lower two strikes typically will have higher premiums.
- There are an equal number of long calls and short calls in the position; therefore, the position has both limited risk and limited reward.

The P&L diagram in **Figure 2.3** illustrates the risk, reward, and breakeven points of the long call butterfly *at expiration*.

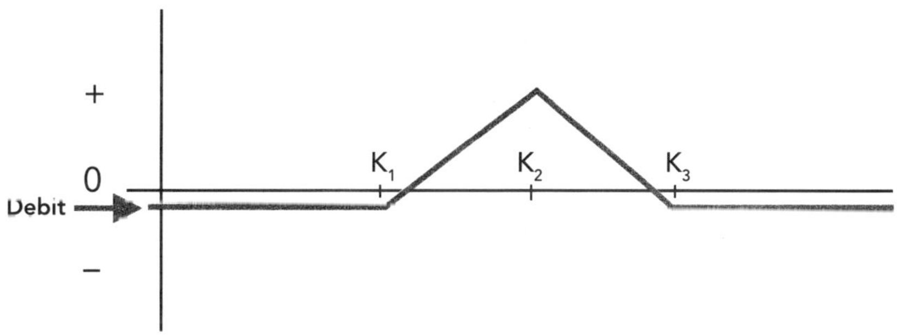

Composition:	Long 1 K_1 call Short 2 K_2 calls Long 1 K_3 call Same expiry, same underlying
Max Profit:	$(K_3 - K_1)/2$ – debit
Max Loss:	Debit
Breakevens:	K_1 + debit; K_3 – debit

Figure 2.3 Long Call Butterfly P&L Diagram *Source: Corona Derivatives, LLC*

Example

Buy the XYZ April 95/100/105 Call Butterfly:

- Buy 1 XYZ April 95 call at $7.00
- Sell 2 XYZ April 100 calls at $4.00
- Buy 1 XYZ April 105 call at $2.00

This creates a long XYZ April 95/100/105 call butterfly at a total cost of $1.00 (–$7 + $8 – $2).

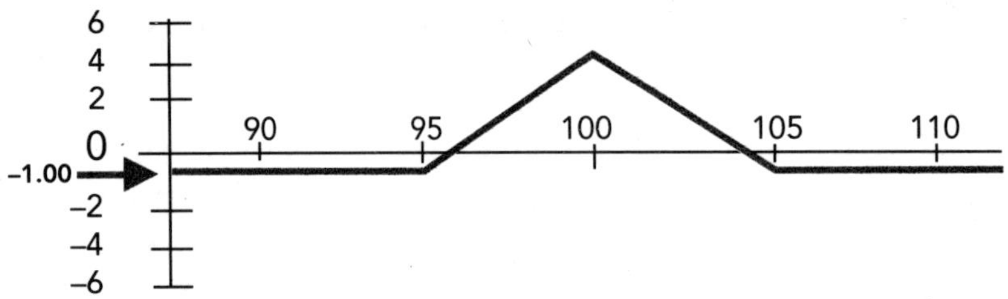

Composition:	Long 1 95 call Short 2 100 calls Long 1 105 call Same expiry, same underlying
Max Profit:	(105 – 95)/2 – 1.00; or 4.00
Max Loss:	1.00
Breakevens:	96.00; 104.00

Figure 2.4 P&L Diagram of the Long XYZ April 95/100/105 Call Butterfly *Source: Corona Derivatives, LLC*

The previous example and **Figure 2.4** illustrate the risk, reward, and break-even points of the long call butterfly *at expiration*. The point of maximum profitability is located at the middle strike *at expiration*; the maximum loss will be realized at or below the lower strike, or at or above the upper strike, *at expiration*. Therefore, at expiration the range of profitability extends from between the lower break-even point, K_1 + debit, and the upper break-even point K_3 – debit.

"What If?" Scenarios (Potential Outcomes at Expiration)

Stock Price of 90.00	Long 1 XYZ April 95 call value	=	$0.00
	Short 2 XYZ April 100 calls value	=	$0.00
	Long 1 XYZ April 105 call value	=	$0.00
	Net value of spread	=	$0.00
	Cost of spread	=	$1.00
	Net profit /loss	**=**	**–$1.00**
Stock Price of 96.00	Long 1 XYZ April 95 call value	=	$1.00
	Short 2 XYZ April 100 calls value	=	$0.00
	Long 1 XYZ April 105 call value	=	$0.00
	Net value of spread	=	$1.00
	Cost of spread	=	$1.00
	Net profit/loss	**=**	**$0.00**
Stock Price of 100.00	Long 1 XYZ April 95 call value	=	$5.00
	Short 2 XYZ April 100 calls value	=	$0.00
	Long 1 XYZ April 105 call value	=	$0.00
	Net value of spread	=	$5.00
	Cost of spread	=	$1.00
	Net profit/loss	**=**	**$4.00**
Stock Price of 104.00	Long 1 XYZ April 95 call value	=	$9.00
	Short 2 XYZ April 100 calls value	=	–$8.00
	Long 1 XYZ April 105 call value	–	$0.00
	Net value of spread	=	$1.00
	Cost of spread	=	$1.00
	Net profit/loss	**=**	**$0.00**
Stock Price of 110.00	Long 1 XYZ April 95 call value	=	$15.00
	Short 2 XYZ April 100 calls value	=	–$20.00
	Long 1 XYZ April 105 call value	=	$5.00
	Net value of spread	=	$0.00
	Cost of spread	=	$1.00
	Net profit/loss	**=**	**—$1.00**

THE PUT BUTTERFLY

Structure

The Put Butterfly uses three strikes of the same expiration cycle and is constructed by purchasing one lower strike (K_1) put, selling two middle strike (K_2) puts, and purchasing one higher strike (K_3) put. (See **Figure 2.5**.) As with the call butterfly, typically the strikes selected are equidistant.

Call	Strike	Put
	K_1	+1
	K_2	–2
	K_3	+1

Figure 2.5 Structure of the Long Put Butterfly Spread
Source: Corona Derivatives, LLC

An inspection of the long put butterfly structure in Figure 2.5 reveals some interesting characteristics of this spread:

- The long put butterfly is a combination of two vertical spreads, a bull spread (short put spread or *credit spread*) combining the lower two strikes, overlapped by a bear spread (long put spread or *debit spread*) combining the upper two strikes. (See **Figure 2.6**.)

Strike	Short Put Spread K_1,K_2	+	Long Put Spread K_2,K_3	=	Long Put Butterfly K_1,K_2,K_3
K_1	+1				+1
K_2	–1		–1		–2
K_3			+1		+1

Figure 2.6 Long Put Butterfly Decomposition Diagram
Source: Corona Derivatives, LLC

- Because the trader is buying the vertical put spread (the upper two strikes) and selling the vertical put spread (the lower two strikes), he usually has to pay for a long put butterfly, since, with puts, the upper two strikes typically will have higher premiums.

- There are an equal number of long puts and short puts in the position; therefore, the position has both limited risk and limited reward.

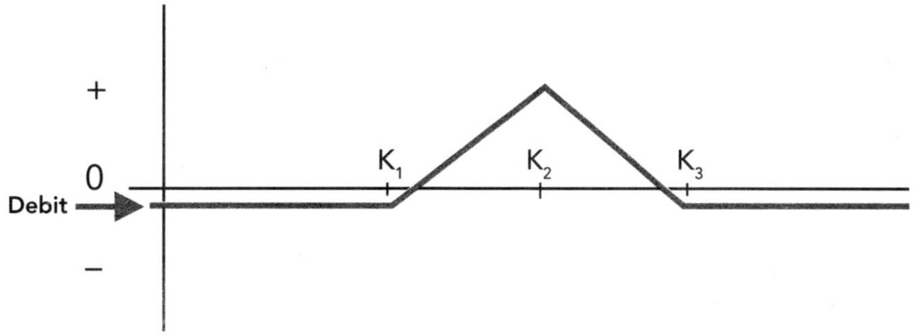

Composition:	Long 1 K_1 put Short 2 K_2 puts Long 1 K_3 put Same expiry, same underlying
Max Profit:	$(K_3 - K_1)/2$ – debit
Max Loss:	Debit
Breakevens:	K_1 + debit; K_3 – debit

Figure 2.7 Long Put Butterfly P&L Diagram *Source: Corona Derivatives, LLC*

Figure 2.7 illustrates the risk, reward, and break-even points of the long put butterfly *at expiration.*

Example

Buy the XYZ April 95/100/105 Put Butterfly:

- Buy 1 XYZ April 95 put at $1.00
- Sell 2 XYZ April 100 puts at $4.50
- Buy 1 XYZ April 105 put at $9.00

This creates a long XYZ April 95/100/105 put butterfly at a total cost of $1.00 (–$1.00 + $9.00 – $9.00).

Figure 2.8 and the previous example illustrate the risk, reward, and break-even points of the long put butterfly at expiration. The point of maximum profitability is located at the middle strike *at expiration,* while the maximum loss will be realized at or below the lower strike or at or above the higher strike *at expiration.* So at expiration, the range of profitability extends from between the lower break-even point, K_1 + debit, and the upper break-even point, K_3 – debit.

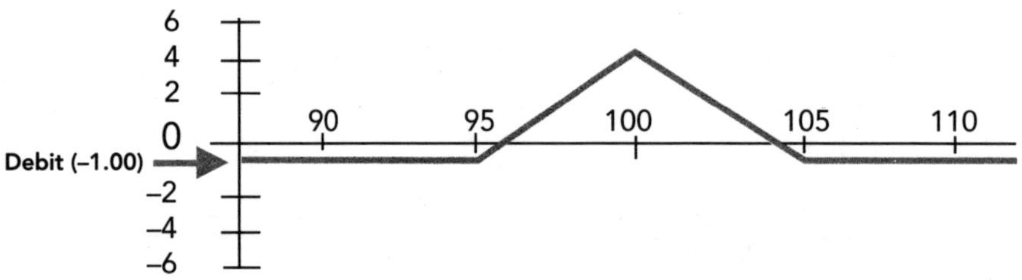

Composition:	Long 1 95 put Short 2 100 puts Long 1 105 put Same expiry, same underlying
Max Profit:	(105 – 95)/2 – 1.00; or 4.00
Max Loss:	1.00
Breakevens:	96.00; 104.00

Figure 2.8 P&L Diagram of the Long XYZ April 95/100/105 Put Butterfly *Source: Corona Derivatives, LLC*

"What If?" Scenarios (Potential Outcomes at Expiration)

Stock Price of 90.00	Long 1 XYZ April 95 put value	=	$5.00
	Short 2 XYZ April 100 puts value	=	–$20.00
	Long 1 XYZ April 105 put value	=	$15.00
	Net value of spread	=	$0.00
	Cost of spread	=	$1.00
	Net profit/loss	**=**	**–$1.00**
Stock Price of 96.00	Long 1 XYZ April 95 put value	=	$0.00
	Short 2 XYZ April 100 puts value	=	–$8.00
	Long 1 XYZ April 105 put value	=	$9.00
	Net value of spread	=	$1.00
	Cost of spread	=	$1.00
	Net profit/loss	**=**	**$0.00**
Stock Price of 100.00	Long 1 XYZ April 95 put value	=	$0.00
	Short 2 XYZ April 100 puts value	=	$0.00
	Long 1 XYZ April 105 put value	=	$5.00
	Net value of spread	=	$5.00

	Cost of spread	=	$1.00
	Net profit/loss	**=**	**$4.00**
Stock Price of 104.00	Long 1 XYZ April 95 put value	=	$0.00
	Short 2 XYZ April 100 puts value	=	$0.00
	Long 1 XYZ April 105 put value	=	$1.00
	Net value of spread	=	$1.00
	Cost of spread	=	$1.00
	Net profit/loss	**=**	**$0.00**
Stock Price of 110.00	Long 1 XYZ April 95 put value	=	$0.00
	Short 2 XYZ April 100 puts value	=	$0.00
	Long 1 XYZ April 105 put value	=	$0.00
	Net value of spread	=	$0.00
	Cost of spread	=	$1.00
	Net profit/loss	**=**	**–$1.00**

P&L BEFORE EXPIRATION AND UNDER CHANGING MARKET CONDITIONS

One of the potential problems faced by investors new to option spread strategies is that most available educational materials use P&L graphs set to expiration day. These hockey-stick graphs can be misleading because they are applicable only at expiration day, when all extrinsic value has vanished. This can be very frustrating for the novice spreader who correctly forecasts the market direction or behavior, but does not realize the profit he or she was expecting because it occurred before expiration or under other market conditions that impacted extrinsic value. For that reason, *at expiration* was heavily emphasized in the preceding P&L diagrams and what-if examples.

As we saw in chapter 1, there are many factors that can affect the extrinsic value of an option, including underlying price, implied volatility, time until expiration, interest rates, dividends, and other factors. The risks associated with these factors are quantified by what are commonly called "the Greeks." To understand how the long butterfly—or any spread strategy—will behave prior to expiration, or under changing market conditions, it is necessary to study the Greeks. Chapters 4 and 5 will be devoted exclusively to understanding the Greeks of the long butterfly and long condor positions, and how they can change as market conditions evolve.

CALL BUTTERFLY OR PUT BUTTERFLY?

It is evident from the preceding P&L diagrams and examples that the risk/reward profiles of the long call butterfly and the long put butterfly (same strikes, same expiration) are identical. Except for a few special situations involving the early exercise of American-style options, there is essentially no difference between the profit and loss scenarios (or risk/reward) of a long call butterfly and a long put butterfly. We will add the long iron butterfly to this list later.

For those butterfly spreads that have identical risk/reward profiles, an investor considering initiating a long butterfly position can choose between buying a call butterfly and buying a put butterfly. Obviously, if they are trading at different prices, one would simply buy the cheaper of the two. Unfortunately, this is a rare occurrence because there are thousands of professional traders (and their computers) monitoring the markets looking for just these types of price discrepancies for possible arbitrage opportunities. The activities of these option arbitrageurs will usually keep the prices of such structures "in line." Be that as it may, it is always a good idea to obtain quotes on both when looking to buy a butterfly, just in case.

Exiting from an existing long call butterfly or long put butterfly position by selling the opposing put or call butterfly may be a bit more problematic for the individual investor. Even though call and put butterflies with the same strikes and same expiration may have identical risk/reward profiles, selling a put butterfly to close an existing long call butterfly position, or selling a call butterfly to close an existing long put butterfly position, leaves a residual position that, though neutral, must be held until expiration.

SUMMARY

In later chapters, we will explore using the butterfly structure as a trading vehicle for more aggressive trading tactics. Some of these tactics include legging into butterfly trades using the individual option or vertical spread subcomponents, incorporating directional or swing trading tactics, and assembling butterflies in stages. When one trades in this fashion the call, put, and iron butterflies may be used interchangeably greatly expanding the arsenal. Factors such as "moneyness" (i.e., whether the options or spreads involved are out-of-the-money, at-the-money, or in-the-money), liquidity, and width of the bid-ask spreads of the component options or spreads may offer a distinct advantage in choosing one butterfly structure over another.

CHAPTER 2 EXERCISE

Consider the option prices in **Figure 2.9** and use them to answer exercise questions 1 through 10.

- *Note that call quotes are on the left and put quotes are on the right.*
- *Buy on the ask and sell on the bid.*

BidSz	Bid	Ask	AskSz	A	Last	T	R	Net	High	Low	Name
2	98.40	99.00	20	P	98.55	-		-0.92	100.75	98.25	XYZ

Net	Last	BBidSize	BBid	BAsk	BAskSize	Strike	pBBidSize	pBBid	pBAsk	pBAskSize	pLast	pNet
24.30	24.30	97	24.10	24.40	73	75.00	200	0.10	0.15	285	0.00	0.00
0.00	0.00	97	19.10	19.60	278	80.00	399	0.15	0.25	26	0.25	-0.18
-0.70	15.00	53	14.40	14.90	308	85.00	10	0.55	0.60	11	0.55	-0.30
-1.20	10.30	31	10.00	10.40	283	90.00	7	1.35	1.45	246	1.40	-0.45
-1.00	6.80	1	6.60	6.80	377	95.00	433	2.80	2.90	20	2.75	-0.65
-1.20	4.00	56	4.00	4.10	434	100.00	469	5.10	5.30	182	5.30	-0.40
-1.00	2.20	267	2.10	2.25	410	105.00	103	8.40	8.60	73	8.00	-0.80
-0.70	1.10	387	1.05	1.15	125	110.00	333	12.20	12.50	75	0.00	0.00
-0.45	0.60	100	0.55	0.60	278	115.00	309	16.60	17.00	105	0.00	0.00
-0.20	0.35	1	0.25	0.30	7	120.00	283	21.30	21.50	20	0.00	0.00
-0.10	0.20	184	0.10	0.20	237	125.00	288	26.10	26.60	74	0.00	0.00
0.00	0.00	4	0.10	0.15	318	130.00	293	31.00	31.50	74	0.00	0.00
0.00	0.00		0.00	0.10	13	135.00	161	36.00	36.40	73	0.00	0.00

Figure 2.9 Option Price Chain for XYZ *Source: LiquidPoint, LLC*

1. What is the composition of the long XYZ July 95/100/105 call butterfly?
2. What price would one pay to initiate the position?
3. What are the break-even points?
4. What is the maximum profit?
5. What is the maximum loss?
6. What does the P&L diagram look like?
7. What is the profit or loss with XYZ stock at 93 at expiration?
8. What is the profit or loss with XYZ stock at 101 at expiration?
9. What is the profit or loss with XYZ stock at 107 at expiration?
10. What is the profit or loss with XYZ stock at 96 at expiration?

CHAPTER 2 QUIZ

1. The butterfly spread can be viewed as two overlapping vertical spreads with the short position sharing the same strike for both verticals. True or false?

2. The long call butterfly can be viewed as a bull call spread overlapped by a bear call spread. True or false?

3. If one is long the XYZ July 60/65/70 call butterfly, one is "buying the wings and selling the body." True or false?

4. What is the formula to determine the maximum profit potential for a long call or a long put butterfly?

For questions 5 through 10, refer to the XYZ Option Price Chain (Figure 2.9).

5. Construct the 75/85/95 long put butterfly and determine the prices of each contract.

6. What is the offer price of the 75/85/95 long put butterfly?

7. What is the maximum profit of the 75/85/95 long put butterfly?

8. What are the break-even points of the 75/85/95 long put butterfly?

9. What is the profit or loss at expiration of the 75/85/95 long put butterfly with the stock at 95?

10. What is your maximum risk?

Chapter 2 Exercise Answer Key

1. Long 1 XYZ 95 call @ $6.80
   Short 2 XYZ 100 calls @ $4.00
   Buy Long 1 XYZ 105 call @ $2.25
2. $1.05 (–$6.80 + $8.00 – $2.25)
3. $96.05 ($K_1$ + debit); $103.95 ($K_3$ – debit)
4. $3.95 ($K_3 - K_1$)/2 – debit
5. $1.05 (debit incurred to initiate spread)
6. 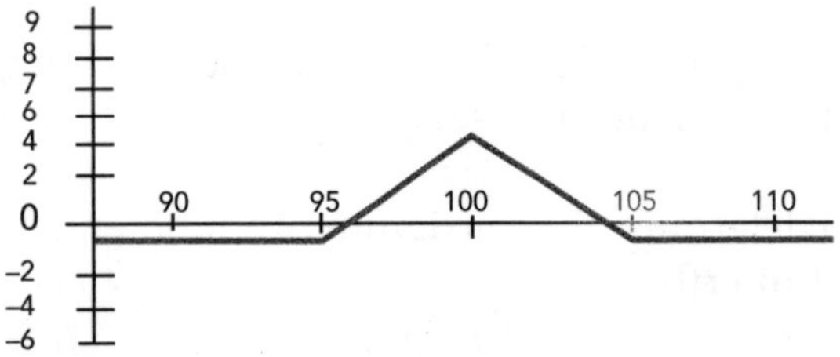

7. The 95 call is worth $0.00, the 100 calls are worth $0.00, and the 105 call is worth $0.00. Therefore, at expiration it would result in a loss of $1.05 (the price paid to initiate it).
8. The 95 call is worth $6.00, the 100 calls are worth $1.00 each, and the 105 call is worth $0.00. Therefore, at expiration it would result in a profit of $2.95 (+$6.00 – $2.00 + $0.00 – $1.05).
9. The 95 call is worth $12.00, the 100 calls are worth $7.00, the 105 call is worth $2.00. Therefore, at expiration it would result in a loss of $1.05 (+$12.00 – $14.00 + $2.00 – $1.05).
10. The 95 call is worth $1.00, the 100 calls are worth $0.00, and the 105 call is worth $0.00. Therefore, at expiration it would result in a loss of $0.05 (+$1.00 – $0.00 –$ 0.00 – $1.05).

Chapter 2 Quiz Answer Key

1. True
2. True
3. True
4. $(K_3 - K_1)/2$ – debit
5. Long 1 XYZ July 75 put @ $0.15
   Short 2 XYZ July 85 puts @ $0.55
   Long 1 XYZ July 95 put @ $2.90
6. $1.95 (–$0.15 + $1.10 – $2.90)
7. $8.05 ($95 – $75)/2 – $1.95
8. $76.95 ($75 + debit), $93.05 ($95 – debit)
9. $1.95 (all puts expire worthless; a $1.95 debit was incurred to initiate the spread)
10. $1.95 (debit incurred to initiate the spread)

3

Long Condor Spread Basics

CONCEPT REVIEW

Directionless market. A period during which prices trade within a narrow range. Also known as a *sideways market.*

American-style option. An option contract that may be exercised on or before expiration.

THE LONG CALL CONDOR

Structure

A long condor is another limited-risk "winged" strategy that can be used to trade a directionless market. Condors are usually lumped into the butterfly family because a condor is really just a variation of the butterfly. A long condor has the same structure as a long butterfly—long the wings, short the body. The difference is that the two short contracts that make up the body of the long condor are distributed over two strikes instead of one. In fact, if one dissects a long condor, one will find two overlapping long butterflies. (See **Figure 3.1**.)

Call	Strike	Put
+1	K_1	
–1	K_2	
–1	K_3	
+1	K_4	

Figure 3.1 Structure of the Long Call Condor Spread
Source: Corona Derivatives, LLC

A condor may be used when one expects a directionless market with a wider trading range, or a trading range that seems to move between the strikes.

A long call condor incorporates four strikes of the same expiration cycle and is constructed by purchasing a lower strike (K_1) call, selling a call at the next two consecutive higher strikes (K_2 and K_3), and purchasing an even higher strike (K_4) call. (See **Figure 3.2.**) Like the long call butterfly, the strikes selected typically are equidistant.

Call Butterfly K_1,K_2,K_3	+	Call Butterfly K_2,K_3,K_4	=	Call Condor K_1,K_2,K_3,K_4	Strike
+1				+1	K_1
–2		+1		–1	K_2
+1		–2		–1	K_3
		+1		+1	K_4

Figure 3.2 Long Call Condor Decomposition Diagram A
Source: Corona Derivatives, LLC

A long call condor is essentially two overlapping long call butterflies, so it shares the characteristics of the long call butterfly:

- The long call condor is a combination of two vertical spreads, a bull spread (long call spread or debit spread combining the lower two strikes) adjacent to a bear spread (short call spread or credit spread combining the upper two strikes). (See **Figure 3.3.**)

Long Call Spread K_1,K_2	+	Short Call Spread K_3,K_4	=	Long Call Condor	Strike	Put
+1				+1	K_1	
–1				–1	K_2	
		–1		–1	K_3	
		+1		+1	K_4	

Figure 3.3 Long Call Condor Decomposition Diagram B
Source: Corona Derivatives, LLC

- Because the trader is buying the vertical call spread (the lowest two strikes) and selling the vertical call spread (the upper two strikes), he usually has to pay for a long call condor, since, with calls, the lower two strikes will typically have higher premiums.

- There are an equal number of long calls and short calls in the position; therefore, the position has both limited risk and limited reward potential.

Figure 3.4 illustrates the risk, reward, and break-even points of the long call condor *at expiration*.

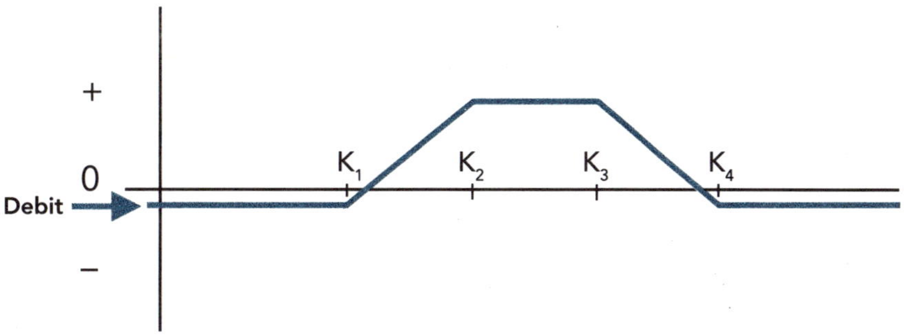

Composition:	Long 1 K_1 call Short 1 K_2 call Short 1 K_3 call Long 1 K_4 call Same expiry, same underlying
Max Profit:	$(K_2 - K_1)$ – debit
Max Loss:	Debit
Breakevens:	K_1 + debit; K_4 – debit

Figure 3.4 Long Call Condor P&L Diagram *Source: Corona Derivatives, LLC*

Example

Buy the XYZ April 95/100/105/110 Call Condor:

- Buy 1 XYZ April 95 call at $7.00
- Sell 1 XYZ April 100 call at $4.00
- Sell 1 XYZ April 105 call at $2.00
- Buy 1 XYZ April 110 call at $1.00

This creates a long XYZ April 95/100/105/110 call condor at a total cost of $2.00.

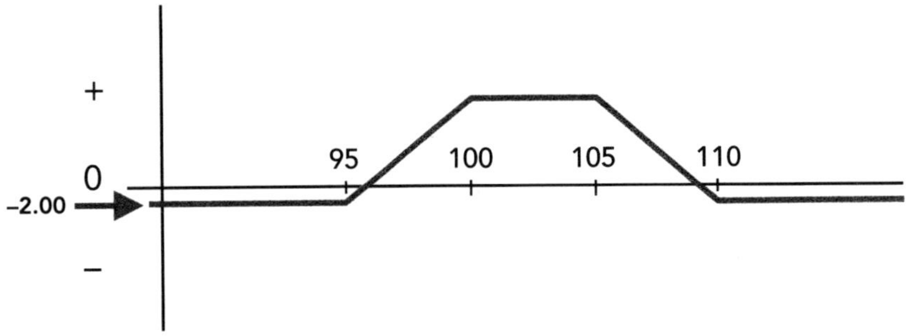

Composition:	Long 1 95 call Short 1 100 call Short 1 105 call Long 1 110 call Same expiry, same underlying
Max Profit:	(100 – 95) – 2.00; or 3.00
Max Loss:	2.00
Breakevens:	97.00; 108.00

Figure 3.5 P&L Diagram of the Long XYZ April 95/100/105/110 Call Condor *Source: Corona Derivatives, LLC*

Figure 3.5 and the preceding example illustrate the risk, reward, and break-even points of the long call condor *at expiration*. Notice that the long condor has an area of maximum profitability as opposed to a point of maximum profitability as with the long call butterfly. The formula to determine the maximum profit potential is $(K_2 - K_1)$ – debit. This area of maximum profitability is located at or between the interior strikes *at expiration*. The maximum loss, equal to the initial debit, will be realized at or below the lower strike, or at or above the upper strike, *at expiration*. So, at expiration, the range of profitability extends from the lower break-even point, K_1 + debit, to the upper break-even point, K_4 – debit.

"What If?" Scenarios (Potential Outcomes at Expiration)

Stock Price of 90.00	Long 1 XYZ April 95 call value	=	$0.00
	Short 1 XYZ April 100 call value	=	$0.00
	Short 1 XYZ April 105 call value	=	$0.00
	Long 1 XYZ April 110 call value	=	$0.00
	Net value of spread	=	$0.00
	Cost of spread	–	$2.00
	Net profit/loss	=	**–$2.00**

Stock Price of 97.00	Long 1 XYZ April 95 call value	=	$2.00
	Short 1 XYZ April 100 call value	=	$0.00
	Short 1 XYZ April 105 call value	=	$0.00
	Long 1 XYZ April 110 call value	=	$0.00
	Net value of spread	=	$2.00
	Cost of spread	=	$2.00
	Net profit/loss	**=**	**$0.00**
Stock Price of 100.00	Long 1 XYZ April 95 call value	=	$5.00
	Short 1 XYZ April 100 call value	=	$0.00
	Short 1 XYZ April 105 call value	=	$0.00
	Long 1 XYZ April 110 call value	=	$0.00
	Net value of spread	=	$5.00
	Cost of spread	=	$2.00
	Net profit/loss	**=**	**$3.00**
Stock Price of 105.00	Long 1 XYZ April 95 call value	=	$10.00
	Short 1 XYZ April 100 call value	=	–$5.00
	Short 1 XYZ April 105 call value	=	$0.00
	Long 1 XYZ April 110 call value	=	$0.00
	Net value of spread	=	$5.00
	Cost of spread	=	$2.00
	Net profit/loss	**=**	**$3.00**
Stock Price of 108.00	Long 1 XYZ April 95 call value	=	$13.00
	Short 1 XYZ April 100 call value	=	–$8.00
	Short 1 XYZ April 105 call value	=	–$3.00
	Long 1 XYZ April 110 call value	=	$0.00
	Net value of spread	=	$2.00
	Cost of spread	=	$2.00
	Net profit/loss	**=**	**$0.00**
Stock Price of 110.00	Long 1 XYZ April 95 call value	=	$15.00
	Short 1 XYZ April 100 call value	=	–$10.00
	Short 1 XYZ April 105 call value	=	–$5.00

Long 1 XYZ April 110 call value	=	\$0.00
Net value of spread	=	\$0.00
Cost of spread	=	\$2.00
Net profit/loss	=	**–\$2.00**

THE LONG PUT CONDOR

Structure

The long put condor also incorporates four strikes of the same expiration cycle and is constructed by purchasing a higher strike (K_4) put, selling a put at the next two consecutive lower strikes (K_3 and K_2), and purchasing a lower strike (K_1) put. (See **Figure 3.6.**) As with the call condor, the strikes selected are usually equidistant.

Call	Strike	Put
	K_1	+1
	K_2	–1
	K_3	–1
	K_4	+1

Figure 3.6 Long Put Condor Spread Structure
Source: Corona Derivatives, LLC

A long put condor is essentially two overlapping long put butterflies, so it shares the general characteristics of the long put butterfly:

Put Butterfly K_1,K_2,K_3	+	Put Butterfly K_2,K_3,K_4	=	Put Condor K_1,K_2,K_3,K_4	Strike
+1				+1	K_1
–2		+1		–1	K_2
+1		–2		–1	K_3
		+1		+1	K_4

Figure 3.7 Long Put Condor Decomposition Diagram A
Source: Corona Derivatives, LLC

The long put condor shares the important characteristics of the long call condor:

- The long put condor is a combination of two vertical spreads, a bear spread (long put spread or debit spread) of the upper two strikes adjacent to a bull spread (short put spread or credit spread) of the lower two strikes. (See **Figure 3.8**.)

Strike	Long Put Spread K_3, K_4	+	Short Put Spread K_1, K_2	=	Long Put Condor
K_1			+1		+1
K_2			−1		−1
K_3	−1				−1
K_4	+1				+1

Figure 3.8 Long Put Condor Decomposition Diagram
Source: Corona Derivatives, LLC

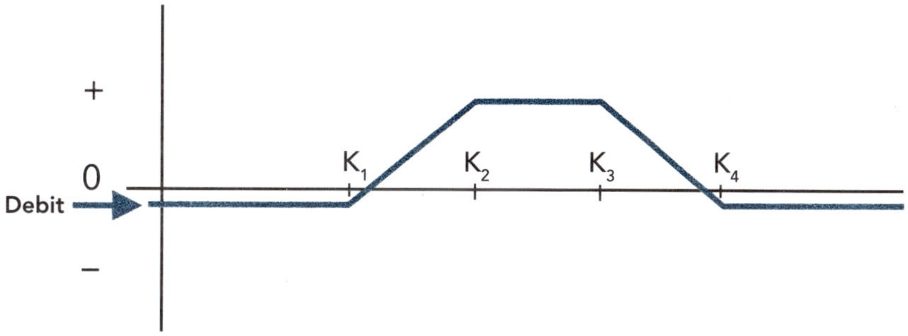

Composition:	Long 1 K_1 put Short 1 K_2 put Short 1 K_3 put Long 1 K_4 put Same expiry, same underlying
Max Profit:	$(K_4 - K_3)$ – debit
Max Loss:	Debit
Breakevens:	K_1 + debit; K_4 – debit

Figure 3.9 P&L Diagram of the Long XYZ Put Condor
Source: Corona Derivatives, LLC

- Because the trader is buying the vertical put spread of the upper two strikes and selling the vertical put spread of the lower two strikes, he usually has to pay for a long put condor.

- There are an equal number of long puts and short puts in the position; therefore, the position has both limited risk and limited reward potential.

The payout diagram in **Figure 3.9** on the previous page illustrates the risk, reward, and break-even points of the long put condor at expiration.

Example

Buy the XYZ April 95/100/105/110 Put Condor:

- Buy 1 XYZ April 95 put at $1.00
- Sell 1 XYZ April 100 put at $4.00
- Sell 1 XYZ April 105 put at $9.50
- Buy 1 XYZ April 110 put at $14.50

This creates a long XYZ April 95/100/105/110 put condor at a total cost of $2.00.

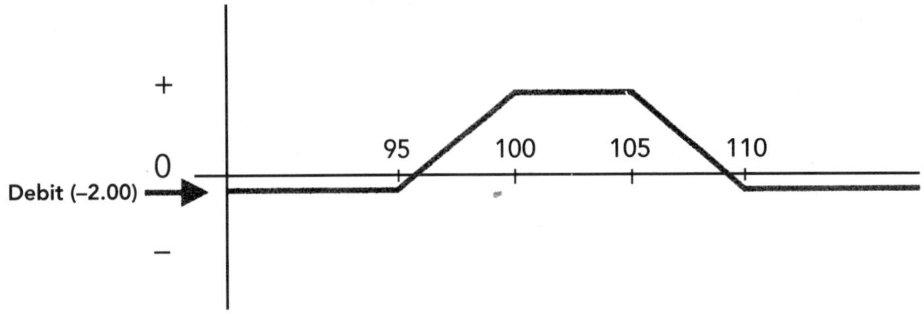

Composition:	Long 1 95 put Short 1 100 put Short 1 105 put Long 1 110 put Same expiry, same underlying
Max Profit:	(110 – 105) – 2.00; or 3.00
Max Loss:	2.00
Breakevens:	97.00; 108.00

Figure 3.10 P&L Diagram of the Long XYZ 95/100/105/110 Put Condor *Source: Corona Derivatives, LLC*

Figure 3.10 and the preceding example illustrate the risk, reward, and break-even points of the long put condor *at expiration*. As with the call condor, the put condor has an area of maximum profitability as opposed to the point of maximum profitability of a long put butterfly. This area of maximum profitability is located at or between the interior strikes *at expiration*. The maximum loss, equal to the initial debit, will be realized at or below the lower strike, or at or above the upper strike, *at expiration*. So, at expiry, the range of profitability extends from the lower break-even point, K_1 + debit, to the upper break-even point, K_4 – debit.

"What If?" Scenarios (Potential Outcomes at Expiration)

Stock Price of 90.00	Long 1 XYZ April 95 put value	=	$5.00
	Short 1 XYZ April 100 put value	=	–$10.00
	Short 1 XYZ April 105 put value	=	–$15.00
	Long 1 XYZ April 110 put value	=	$20.00
	Net value of spread	=	$0.00
	Cost of spread	=	$2.00
	Net profit/loss	**=**	**–$2.00**
Stock Price of 97.00	Long 1 XYZ April 95 put value	=	$0.00
	Short 1 XYZ April 100 put value	=	–$3.00
	Short 1 XYZ April 105 put value =		–$8.00
	Long 1 XYZ April 110 put value	=	$13.00
	Net value of spread	=	$2.00
	Cost of spread	=	$2.00
	Net profit/loss	**=**	**$0.00**
Stock Price of 100.00	Long 1 XYZ April 95 put value	=	$0.00
	Short 1 XYZ April 100 put value	=	$0.00
	Short 1 XYZ April 105 put value	=	–$5.00
	Long 1 XYZ April 110 put value	=	$10.00
	Net value of spread	=	$5.00
	Cost of spread	=	$2.00
	Net profit/loss	**=**	**$3.00**
Stock Price of 105.00	Long 1 XYZ April 95 put value	=	$0.00
	Short 1 XYZ April 100 put value	=	$0.00
	Short 1 XYZ April 105 put value	=	$0.00
	Long 1 XYZ April 110 put value	=	$5.00
	Net value of spread	=	$5.00
	Cost of spread	=	$2.00
	Net profit/loss	**=**	**$3.00**

Stock Price of 108.00	Long 1 XYZ April 95 put value	=	$0.00
	Short 1 XYZ April 100 put value	=	$0.00
	Short 1 XYZ April 105 put value	=	$0.00
	Long 1 XYZ April 110 put value	=	$2.00
	Net value of spread	=	$2.00
	Cost of spread	=	$2.00
	Net profit/loss	**=**	**$0.00**
Stock Price of 110.00	Long 1 XYZ April 95 put value	=	$0.00
	Short 1 XYZ April 100 put value	=	$0.00
	Short 1 XYZ April 105 put value	=	$0.00
	Long 1 XYZ April 110 put value	=	$0.00
	Net value of spread	=	$0.00
	Cost of spread	=	$2.00
	Net profit/loss	**=**	**–$2.00**

CALL CONDOR OR PUT CONDOR?

As with the call and put butterflies, it is clear that, given the same effective price, the risk/reward profiles of the long call and put condor (same strikes, same expiry) are identical except for a few special situations involving the early exercise of American-style options. There is essentially no difference between a long call condor and a long put condor. As with the long call and put butterflies, we will explore why one might prefer to use one type of long condor over another when we examine trading tactics.

SUMMARY

A long condor is a variation of the long butterfly strategy that allows for coverage of an underlying stock or index that is moving sideways within a wider trading range, or seems to be bouncing between strike prices. In these cases, a long butterfly would give inadequate coverage, and the wider area of potential profitability of the long condor is required to cover the zone in which the underlying is moving. (See **Figure 3.11**.)

Stretching the body of the structure over two strikes rather than one provides a larger range of profitability that can help cover the wider trading range. This extra coverage is not free. A condor, because it is two butterflies, is more expensive than a butterfly. The extra premium spent buying a condor rather than a butterfly buys a larger range of profitability, but maximum profit is decreased and maximum loss is increased, by this amount. (See **Figure 3.12**.)

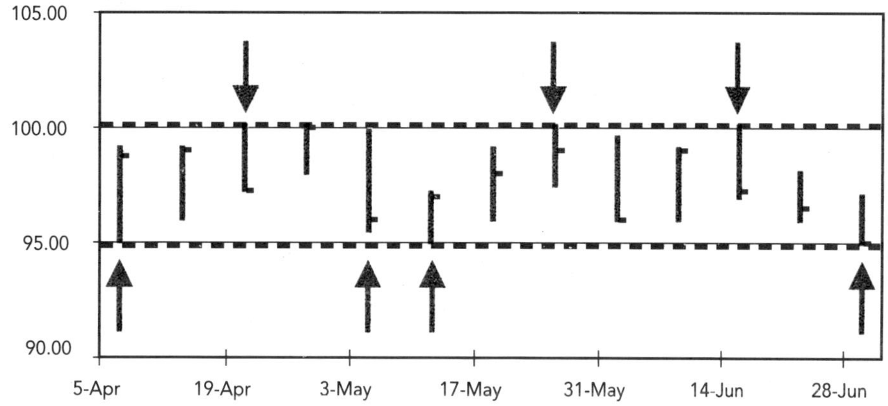

Figure 3.11 Trading Range *Source: Corona Derivatives, LLC*

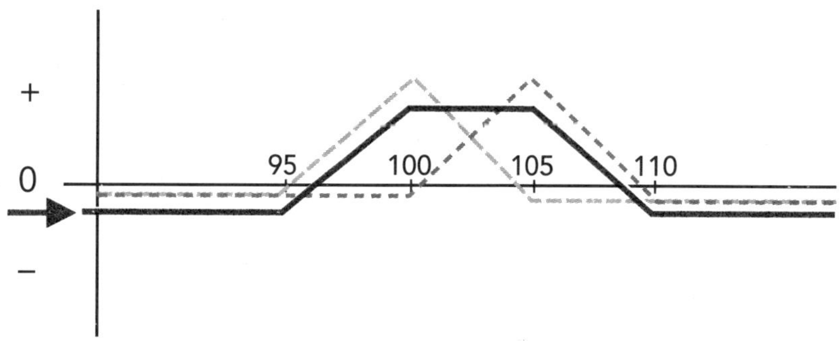

Figure 3.12 Butterfly–Condor Comparison *Source: Corona Derivatives, LLC*

CHAPTER 3 EXERCISE

Consider the option prices in **Figure 3.13** and use them to answer exercise questions 1 through 10.

- *Note that call quotes are on the left and put quotes are on the right.*
- *Buy on the ask and sell on the bid.*

BidSz	Bid	Ask	AskSz	A	Last	T	R	Net	High	Low	Name
11	74.64	74.66	3	N	74.66	-		0.12	74.89	74.40	XYZ

Net	Last	BBidSize	BBid	BAsk	BAskSize	Strike	pBBidSize	pBBid	pBAsk	pBAskSize	pLast	pNet
0.00	0.00	734	19.60	19.80	737	55.00		0.00	0.05	4,235	0.00	0.00
0.00	0.00	943	14.60	14.80	856	60.00		0.00	0.05	4,192	0.00	0.00
0.00	0.00	938	9.60	9.80	892	65.00		0.00	0.05	3,696	0.00	0.00
-0.50	4.50	1,714	4.60	4.80	935	70.00		0.00	0.05	4,568	0.00	0.00
0.00	0.40	6,385	0.30	0.40	4,113	75.00	2,447	0.60	0.70	4,806	0.65	-0.05
0.00	0.00		0.00	0.05	3,053	80.00	1,012	5.20	5.50	1,022	0.00	0.00
0.00	0.00		0.00	0.05	5,365	85.00	973	10.20	10.50	964	0.00	0.00
0.00	0.00		0.00	0.05	4,754	90.00	957	15.20	15.50	974	0.00	0.00
0.00	0.00		0.00	0.05	4,282	95.00	973	20.20	20.50	965	0.00	0.00
0.00	0.00		0.00	0.05	4,178	100.00	977	25.20	25.50	960	0.00	0.00
0.00	0.00		0.00	0.05	3,551	105.00	977	30.20	30.50	966	0.00	0.00

Figure 3.13 Option Price Chain for XYZ *Source: LiquidPoint, LLC*

1. What is the composition of the long XYZ 60/65/70/75 call condor?
2. What price would one pay to initiate the position?
3. What are the break-even points?
4. What is the maximum profit?
5. What is the maximum loss?
6. What does the P&L diagram look like?
7. What is the profit or loss with XYZ stock at 63 at expiration?
8. What is the profit or loss with XYZ stock at 68 at expiration?
9. What is the profit or loss with XYZ stock at 76 at expiration?
10. What is the profit or loss with XYZ stock at 59 at expiration?

CHAPTER 3 QUIZ

1. The maximum loss on the trade will be realized at or below the lower strike, or at or above the upper strike. True or false?

2. The long call condor has two overlapping long call butterflies. True or false?

3. The breakevens for the long put condor are K_1 – debit and K_4 + debit. True or false?

4. The long put condor is also a combination of two vertical spreads, a bear spread of the lower two strikes adjacent to a bull spread of the higher two strikes. True or false?

For quiz questions 5 through 10, refer to the XYZ Option Price Chain in **Figure 3.14**.

- *Note that call quotes are on the left and put quotes are on the right.*
- *Buy on the ask and sell on the bid.*

BidSz	Bid	Ask	AskSz	A	Last	T	R	Net	High	Low	Name
11	74.64	74.66	3	N	74.66	-		0.12	. 74.89	. 74.40	XYZ

Net	Last	BBidSize	BBid	BAsk	BAskSize	Strike	pBBidSize	pBBid	pBAsk	pBAskSize	pLast	pNet
0.00	0.00	734	19.60	19.80	737	55.00		0.00	0.05	4,235	0.00	0.00
0.00	0.00	943	14.60	14.80	856	60.00		0.00	0.05	4,192	0.00	0.00
0.00	0.00	938	9.60	9.80	892	65.00		0.00	0.05	3,696	0.00	0.00
-0.50	4.50	1,714	4.60	4.80	935	70.00		0.00	0.05	4,568	0.00	0.00
0.00	0.40	6,385	0.30	0.40	4,113	75.00	2,447	0.60	0.70	4,806	0.65	-0.05
0.00	0.00		0.00	0.05	3,053	80.00	1,012	5.20	5.50	1,022	0.00	0.00
0.00	0.00		0.00	0.05	5,365	85.00	973	10.20	10.50	964	0.00	0.00
0.00	0.00		0.00	0.05	4,754	90.00	957	15.20	15.50	974	0.00	0.00
0.00	0.00		0.00	0.05	4,282	95.00	973	20.20	20.50	965	0.00	0.00
0.00	0.00		0.00	0.05	4,178	100.00	977	25.20	25.50	960	0.00	0.00
0.00	0.00		0.00	0.05	3,551	105.00	977	30.20	30.50	966	0.00	0.00

Figure 3.14 Option Price Chain for XYZ *Source: LiquidPoint, LLC*

5. Construct the 80/85/90/95 long put condor and determine the prices of each contract.

6. What is the offer price of the 80/85/90/95 long put condor?

7. What is the maximum profit of the 80/85/90/95 long put condor?

8. What are the break-even points of the 80/85/90/95 long put condor?

9. What is the profit or loss at expiration of the 80/85/90/95 long put condor with the stock at 91?

10. What is the maximum risk of the 80/85/90/95 long put condor?

Chapter 3 Exercise Answer Key

1. Long 1 XYZ 60 @ \$14.80
   Short 1 XYZ 65 @ \$9.60
   Short 1 XYZ 70 @ \$4.60
   Long 1 XYZ 75 @ \$0.40
2. \$1.00 (–\$14.80 + \$9.60 + \$4.60 – \$0.40)
3. \$61 (K_1 + debit); \$74 (K_4 – debit)
4. \$4.00 ($K_2 - K_1$) – debit
5. \$1.00 (debit incurred to initiate spread)
6. 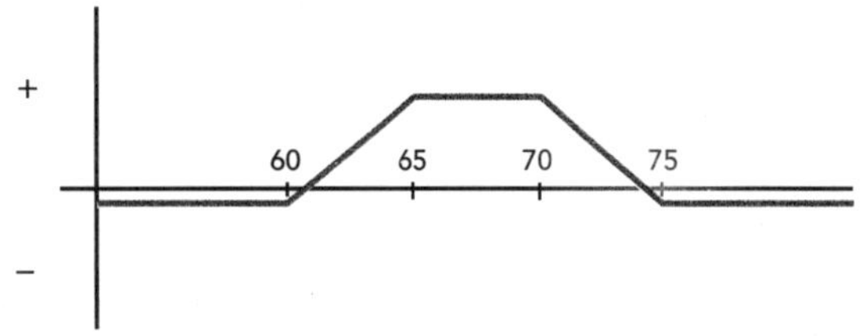

7. The 60 call is worth \$3.00, the 65 call is worth \$0.00, the 70 call is worth \$0.00, and the 75 call is worth \$0.00. Therefore, at expiration it would result in a profit of \$2.00 (+\$3.00 – \$0.00 – \$.0.00 + \$0.00 – \$1.00).
8. The 60 call is worth \$8.00, the 65 call is worth \$3.00, the 70 call is worth \$0.00, and the 75 call is worth \$0.00. Therefore, at expiration it would result in a profit of \$4.00 (+\$8.00 – \$3.00 – \$0.00 + \$0.00 – \$1.00).
9. The 60 call is worth \$16.00, the 65 call is worth \$11.00, the 70 call is worth \$6.00, and the 75 call is worth \$1.00. Therefore, at expiration it would result in a loss of \$1.00 (+\$16.00 – \$11.00 – \$6.00 + \$1.00 – \$1.00).
10. The 60 call is worth \$0.00, the 65 call is worth \$0.00, the 70 call is worth \$0.00, and the 75 call is worth \$0.00. Therefore, at expiration it would result in a loss of \$1.00 (+\$0.00 – \$0.00 – \$0.00 + \$0.00 – \$1.00).

Chapter 3 Quiz Answer Key

1. True
2. True
3. False (K_1 + debit, K_4 – debit)
4. False. The long put condor is also a combination of two vertical spreads, a bear spread of the upper two strikes adjacent to a bull spread of the lower two strikes.
5. Long 1 XYZ 80 put @ $5.50
   Short 1 XYZ 85 put @ $10.20
   Short 1 XYZ 90 put @ $15.20
   Long 1 XYZ 95 put @ $20.50
6. $0.60 (–$5.50 + $10.20 + $15.20 – $20.50)
7. $4.40 ($K_4$ – K_3 – debit)
8. $80.60 ($K_1$ + debit); $94.40 ($K_4$ – debit)
9. The 80 put is worth $0.00, the 85 put is worth $0.00, the 90 put is worth $0.00, and the 95 put is worth $4.00. Therefore, at expiration it would result in a profit of $3.40. (+$0.00 – $0.00 – $0.00 + $4.00 – $0.60).
10. $0.60 (debit incurred to initiate the spread)

4

The Greeks

CONCEPT REVIEW

Implied volatility. It is derived from current option prices and can be viewed as the market's forecast of the average volatility through the remaining life of the option.

Historical volatility. It measures the price fluctuations of an underlying instrument over a given period of time.

Delta. The sensitivity (rate of change) of an option's theoretical value (assessed value) to a $1 move of the underlying instrument. Delta is the probability that the option will expire in-the-money.

Gamma. The sensitivity (rate of change) of an option's delta with respect to a $1 move in the underlying's price.

Theta. The sensitivity (rate of change) of theoretical option prices with regard to small changes in time. Theta measures the rate of decay in the time value of options. Often, theta is expressed as the amount of erosion of an option's theoretical value over one day in time.

Vega. The sensitivity (rate of change) of an option's theoretical value to a change in implied volatility. Often, vega is expressed as the number of points of theoretical value gained or lost from a 1 percent rise or fall in implied volatility.

- **Author's Note**

In order to better illustrate the behavior of the Greeks with respect to time and volatility, Figures 4.5, 4.7, 4.8, and 4.9 have the scale of the *x* axes adjusted to emphasize the behavior of the Greeks as time and/or implied volatility approach zero.

LONG CALL BUTTERFLY AND CONDOR PLACEMENT

When using a long butterfly or condor spread to trade the directionless market, the idea is to fit the range of profitability over the projected trading range, and to place the middle strike(s) of the structure where one expects the underlying to be at expiration. If one's forecast is correct and the underlying continues to move sideways, time decay will eat away at the extrinsic value of the options in the position, causing the butterfly/condor price to expand. At expiration, the extrinsic value of the options is gone, leaving only intrinsic value, if any.

It is the loss of extrinsic value through time decay that causes the correctly placed butterfly/condor to expand in value. As expiration approaches and time decay for the at-the-money options accelerates, the price expansion of the butterfly/condor also accelerates toward its textbook P&L diagram. (See **Figure 4.1**.)

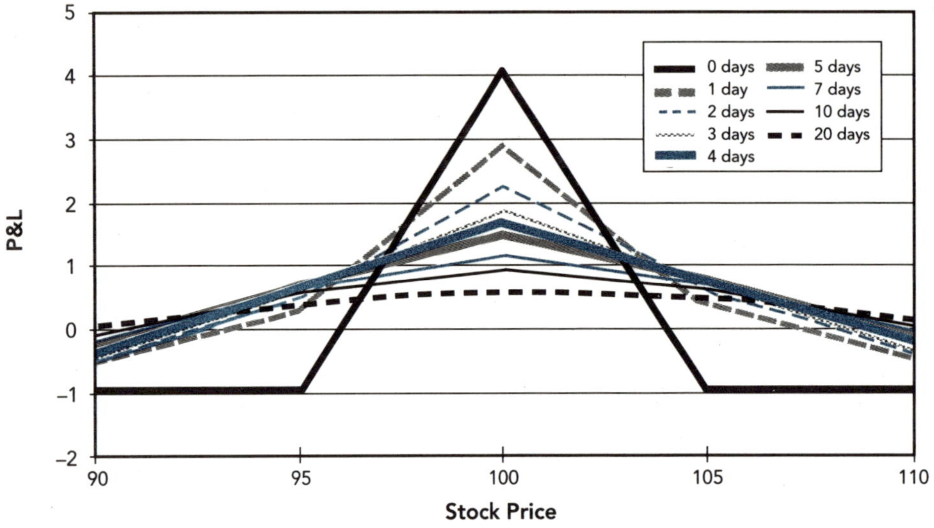

Figure 4.1 Long Butterfly Spread vs. Time
Source: Corona Derivatives, LLC

As noted in Chapter 2, for each option series, expiration comes only once, and the expansion graphic in Figure 4.1 illustrates one of the problems faced by investors new to options or specific options strategies—most P&L graphs of options strategies are set to expiration only after all extrinsic value is gone. The actual price behavior of a long butterfly/condor position any time before expiration, or under other changing market conditions, can be quite different from its price behavior at expiration. This can result in a frustrating disconnect between expectations and reality for the novice spread trader. One way to determine how a long butterfly/condor position (or any other position) may likely behave under changing market conditions is to study the partial derivatives, commonly known as *the Greeks*.

PRICING MODELS

The Greeks may be used to describe the sensitivity of an option's theoretical price to changes in a number of market conditions, and to help a trader anticipate how changing market conditions might impact the value of his position. Also, it is important to note that a change in any of the market conditions will likely result in a change in all of the Greeks of a position.

Basic pricing models calculate the theoretical price of an option based on six inputs used to describe market conditions:

- Underlying Price
- Strike Price
- Time to Expiration
- Interest Rates
- Dividends (if any)
- Implied Volatility

THE GREEKS

Delta

Delta describes the sensitivity (rate of change) of an option's price to changes in the option's underlying's price. Expressed as a percentage, it represents an equivalent amount of the underlying at a given moment in time. Calls are assigned a positive delta (call option prices are positively correlated with the underlying price); puts are assigned a negative delta (put option prices are negatively correlated with the underlying price).

From a practical standpoint, perhaps the best way to view the delta of an option is as *the probability that the option will expire in-the-money*. This may help one to visualize how the delta of an option or the delta of a position may change as underlying conditions change. The delta of an option has everything to do with moneyness (whether the option is in-, at-, or out-of-the-money), *and the probability that it will stay there through expiration.*

The delta of an underlying can be considered 1 (100 percent). This makes sense because if one is long XYZ stock and it increases by $1.00, then the owner would realize a $1.00 profit. Therefore, if the XYZ May 100 calls have a delta of 50, this means that for every $1.00 move in XYZ stock, the May 100 calls' premium will change by $0.50 (or 50 percent of the movement of the stock).

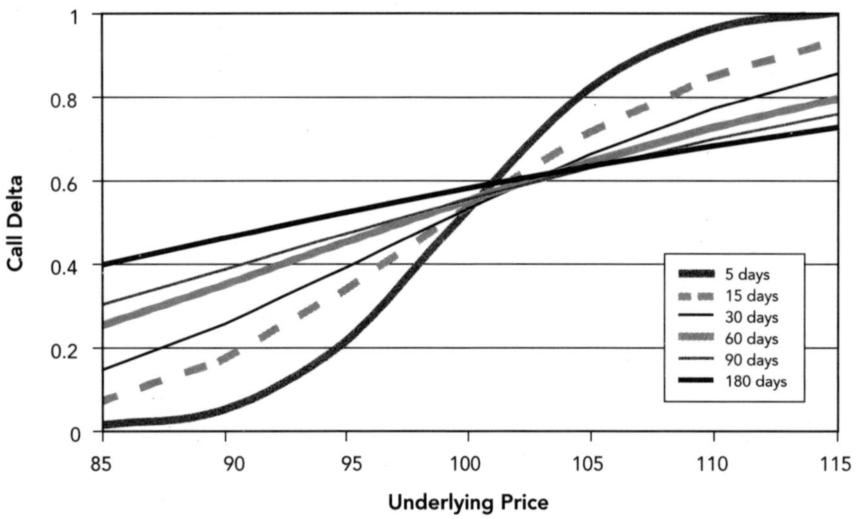

Figure 4.2 Call Delta vs. Underlying Price [Strike = 100]
Source: Corona Derivatives, LLC

Figure 4.2 charts the delta of a call with a strike price of 100 (i.e., a 100 call) versus various underlying prices and different expiration dates. As can be seen from the chart, the delta of a call option can range between 0.00 and 1.00 (the percent sign is usually dropped for the decimal equivalent) and is approximately 0.50 when it is at-the-money (stock price = strike price).

Figure 4.3 charts the delta of a put with a strike price of 100 (i.e., a 100 put) versus various underlying prices and different expiration dates. As can be seen from the chart, the delta of a put option can range between 0.00 and –1.00, and is approximately –0.50 when it is at-the-money (stock price = strike price).

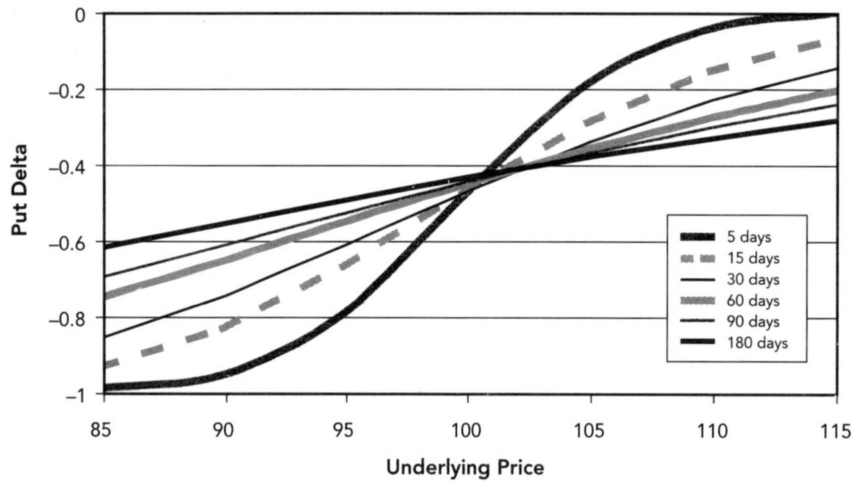

Figure 4.3 Put Delta vs. Underlying Price [Strike = 100]
Source: Corona Derivatives, LLC

Figures 4.2 and 4.3 also illustrate how the delta of an option is dependent on time until expiration. The more time until expiration, the less sensitive the delta of an option is to changes in price. For example, in Figure 4.2, the delta of a 100 call with 180 days until expiration at an underlying price of 105.00 is approximately 0.60, whereas the delta of a 100 call with five days until expiration at the same underlying price of 105 is approximately 0.80. Remember, the delta of an option is the probability that the option will expire in-the-money. When there is a lot of time left until expiration, there is more time for the underlying price to change and affect the outcome as to whether an option finishes in-the-money or out-of-the money, so the probability of the 180-day 100 call finishing in the money is only 0.60, whereas with fewer remaining trading days the probability of the five-day 100 call finishing in-the-money is 0.80 (with an underlying price of 105).

Thinking in terms of possible outcomes at expiration and the way that the expansion of possible price outcomes (more time until expiration, higher volatility) or the contraction of possible price outcomes (less time until expiration, lower volatility) affects the sensitivity of options is very important for understanding the behavior of spread positions. **Figure 4.4** illustrates another example.

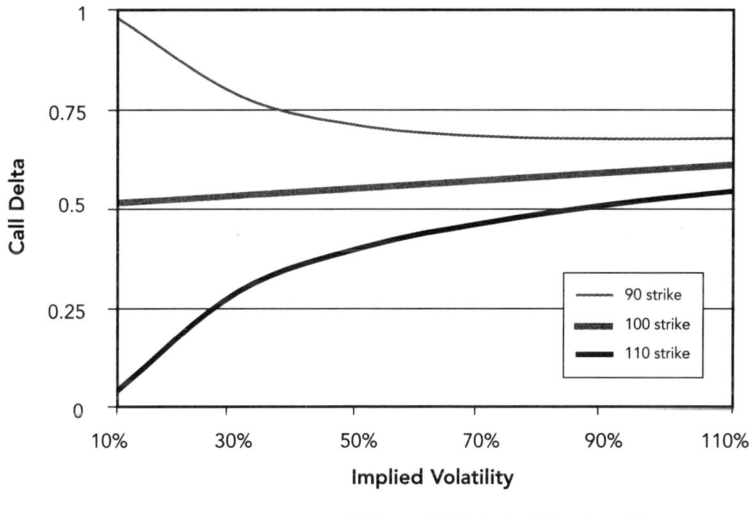

Figure 4.4 Call Delta vs. Implied Volatility [Stock price = 100; 90 days to expiration] *Source: Corona Derivatives, LLC*

Charting the delta of the 90, 100, and 110 calls versus changes in implied volatility (stock price fixed at $100.00; days until expiration fixed at 90) shows how the delta of an option responds to declining implied volatility (a contraction of possible outcomes).

Working from right to left, we can see how declining implied volatility causes the delta of the in-the-money 90 calls to move up toward 1.00, while the delta of the out-of-the-money 110 calls drops toward 0.00. The delta of the at-the-money calls will remain near 0.50 because it cannot be known whether they will finish in- or out-of-the-money until the last moment before expiration.

• **Summary**

By viewing the delta of an option as the probability that the option may expire in-the-money, it is easier to visualize how changing market conditions will affect the delta of an option. Conditions causing an expansion of possible price outcomes, such as more time until expiration or higher implied volatility, will cause the delta of in-the-money options to fall and the delta of out-of-the-money options to rise, while a contraction of possible price outcomes, such as less time until expiration or lower implied volatility, will cause the delta of in-the-money options to rise and the delta of out-of-the-money options to fall.

Gamma

Gamma represents the sensitivity (rate of change) of an option's delta with respect to changes in the underlying's price. The convention is to express gamma in terms of the change in delta produced by a 1-point move in the underlying. For example, if the delta of a 100 call changed from 0.50 to 0.60 as the underlying moved from 100.00 to 101.00, it would be said to have a gamma of 0.10. Long option positions have a positive gamma and short option positions have a negative gamma. The absolute value of the gamma will be identical with call and put options of the same strike and expiration.

As demonstrated in figures 4.2 and 4.3, the sensitivity of the delta is dependent on time until expiration, and the greatest sensitivity occurs when the underlying is at the strike price (the option is at-the-money). **Figure 4.5** charts the gamma of the 90, 100, and 110 call options against time until expiration, stock price set at 100.00 with implied volatility set to 50 percent. Note the close relationship between the gammas of the different strikes when

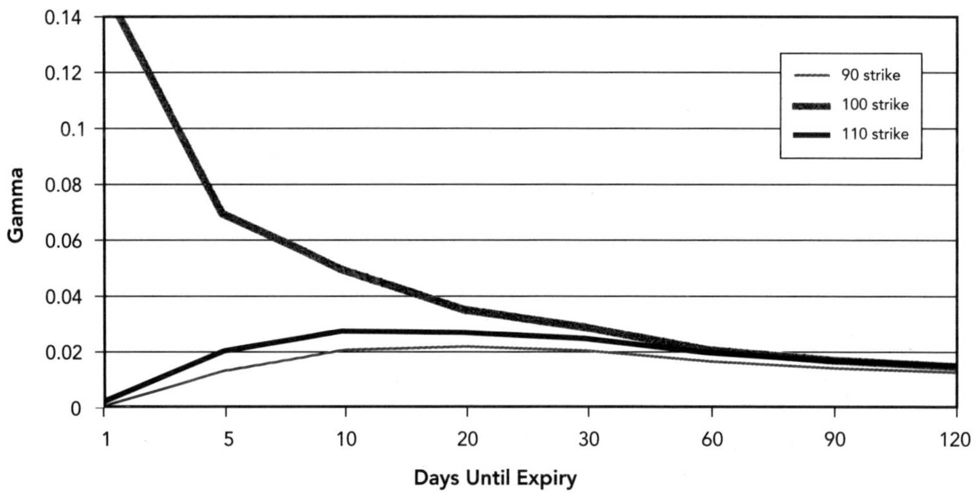

Figure 4.5 Gamma vs. Time to Expiry [Stock price = 100; implied volatility = 0.50] *Source: Corona Derivatives, LLC*

there is a long time until expiration, and how this relationship differs as time passes.

Once again, thinking in terms of possible outcomes at expiration may help one to understand gamma. If the delta is the probability of an option expiring in-the-money, it follows that the gamma would not be very sensitive when there is a long time until expiration because there is still plenty of time for the underlying to move and affect the outcome. At the 120-day point, the gamma of the 90 calls (in-the-money), the 100 calls (at-the-money), and the 110 calls (out-of-the-money) are fairly close. There is such a long time until expiration that their delta sensitivities are very similar.

As time moves forward toward expiration and the underlying price remains at 100, the delta of the in-the-money option begins to move toward 1.00, and the delta of the out-of-the-money option begins to move toward 0.00. In addition, the deltas of these options begin to lose their sensitivity to changes in the underlying price as their outcomes start to become more likely. The gamma of the in-the-money and out-of-the-money options drops as expiration approaches.

The gamma of the at-the-money strike rises sharply as expiration approaches. The delta of an at-the-money option near expiration is very sensitive because the slightest move in the underlying price can put it either in-the-money or out-of-the-money, with $0.02 moves in the underlying possibly taking the delta from 0.00 to 1.00 and back again. **Figure 4.6** illustrates how gamma flows out of the in-the-money and out-of-the-money options and into the at-the-money options as time passes.

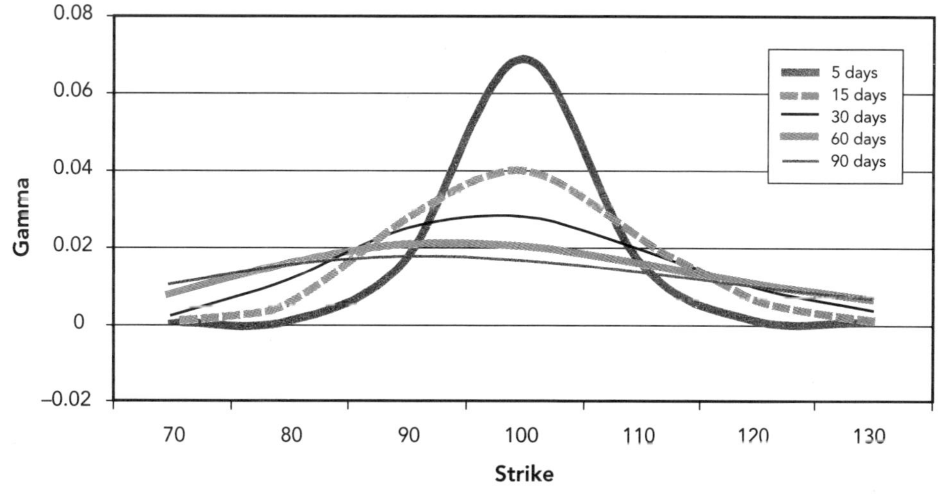

Figure 4.6 Gamma vs. Strike Price [Stock price = 100]
Source: Corona Derivatives, LLC

How do changes in implied volatility affect the gamma of an option? Remember that rising volatility causes an expansion of possible price outcomes—like running the clock in reverse and increasing time until expiration—and it has the same effect on gamma (i.e., the gamma of the at-the-money option will fall to a level similar to the gamma of in-the-money and out-of-the-money options because the outcome is becoming less clear). Falling volatility causes a contraction in possible price outcomes—like fast-forwarding the clock and decreasing time until expiration—and it has the same effect on gamma (i.e., the gamma of the at-the-money option will rise while the gamma of in-the-money and out-of-the-money options will drop because the outcome is becoming clearer).

Note the similarity between **Figure 4.7**, "Gamma vs. Implied Volatility," and Figure 4.5, "Gamma vs. Time to Expiry."

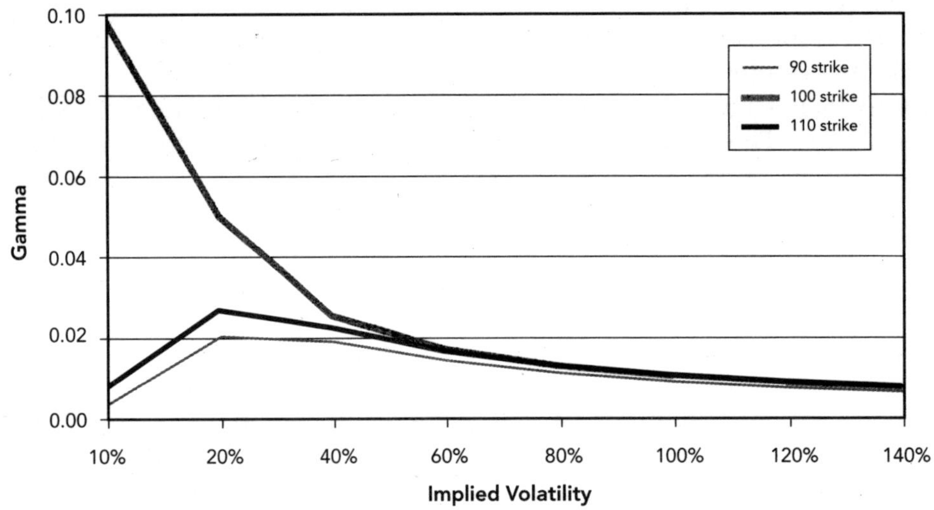

Figure 4.7 Gamma vs. Implied Volatility *Source: Corona Derivatives, LLC*

- **Summary**

Gamma describes the sensitivity of the delta to changes in the option's underlying's price. At-the-money options have the highest gamma, and, as expiration approaches, the gamma of the at-the-money option will rise sharply while the gamma of in-the-money and out-of-the-money options will drop. Falling implied volatility will have an effect similar to the passage of time on gamma, while rising implied volatility mimics the clock running in reverse and causes the gamma of the at-the-money option to drop and the gamma of the in- and out-of the-money options to rise.

Vega

Vega describes the sensitivity of an option's theoretical value to a change in implied volatility. It is usually expressed in the number of points of theoretical value that would be gained or lost from a 1 percent rise or fall in implied volatility. Long option positions have a positive vega, and short option positions have a negative vega. The absolute value of the vega will be identical with call and put options of the same strike and expiration.

Because options have an asymmetrical payout (i.e., they can never go below zero), rising implied volatility causes the extrinsic value of options to rise, and falling implied volatility causes the extrinsic value of options to fall. Longer-dated options are more sensitive to changes in implied volatility, as a projected rise or fall of implied volatility over a longer period is extrapolated to a much larger (in the case of rising volatility) or much smaller (in the case of falling volatility) universe of possible price outcomes at expiration. This is illustrated in **Figure 4.8**.

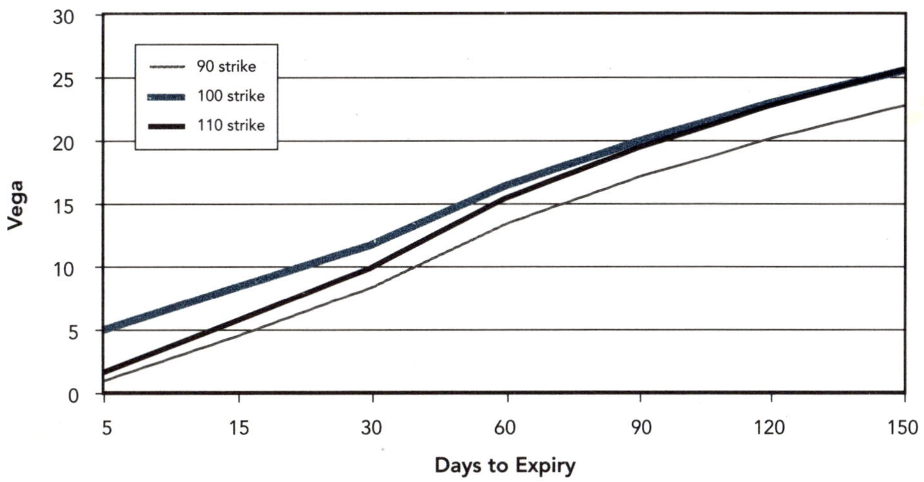

Figure 4.8 Vega vs. Time to Expiry [Stock price = 100]
Source: Corona Derivatives, LLC

Notice the inverse relationship between the vega of an option and time until expiration. It is also important to note that the at-the-money options, will have the highest vega, and that the vega of the in-the-money and out-of-the-money options will drop off faster than the at-the-money options as expiration approaches.

- **Summary**

Vega describes the sensitivity of an option's theoretical price to a 1 percent change in implied volatility. Vega of at-the-money options will be higher than that of in-the-money or out-of-the-money options, and increasing time to expiration will increase the sensitivity of an option's theoretical value to changes in implied volatility.

Theta

As discussed in Chapter 1, theta is used to describe the sensitivity of an option's theoretical value to the passage of time. It is usually expressed as the number of points of theoretical value that are lost from one day's time decay. Long option positions have a negative theta, and short option positions have a positive theta. The absolute value of the theta will be identical with call and put options of the same strike and expiration. Prior to expiration, all options are composed of intrinsic value and extrinsic value, and as time passes, the extrinsic value begins to decay. At expiration the extrinsic value is gone, and an option is either in-the-money and has intrinsic value, or expires worthless. The rate at which extrinsic value decays is not linear and is itself dependent on other market factors, especially time to expiration, as can be seen in **Figure 4.9**.

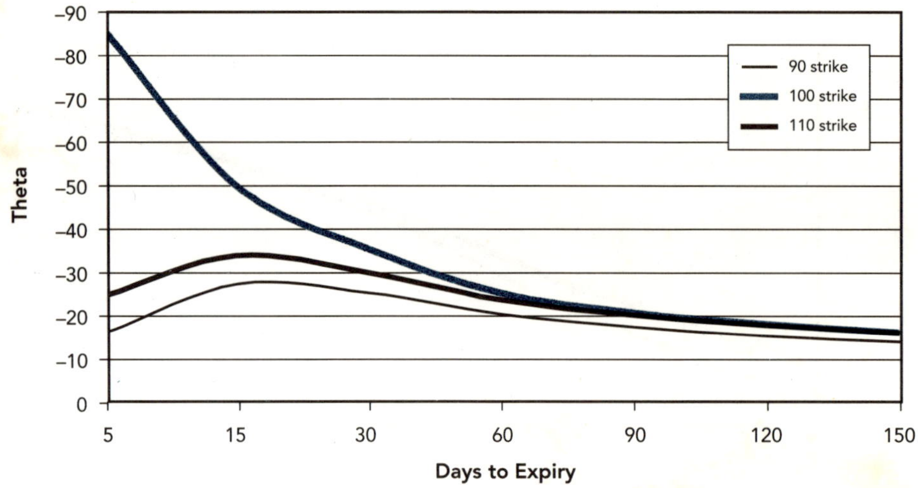

Figure 4.9 Theta vs. Time to Expiry [Stock price = 100]
Source: Corona Derivatives, LLC

The time decay of long-dated options is low and is very similar between the 90, 100, and 110 calls. As time moves toward expiration, time decay begins to accelerate and the theta for all of the options begins to rise. Then, as expiration approaches, the in-the-money and out-of-the-money options begin to lose their extrinsic value and their thetas begin to decline, but the theta of the at-the-money option, which is the highest-priced option that is composed entirely of extrinsic value, begins to accelerate. When expiration is imminent, the surrounding in-the-money and out-of-the-money options have little extrinsic value to lose, and the decay of the at-the-money option will continue to accelerate. Notice the similarity between Figure 4.9, "Theta vs. Time to Expiry," and Figure 4.5, "Gamma vs. Time to Expiry."

- **Summary**

Theta describes the sensitivity of an option's theoretical price to the passage of one day in time. Long-dated options have less sensitivity to the passage of time than short-dated options. Although at-the-money options will always have the highest theta because they have the greatest extrinsic value, as expiration approaches, the theta of the at-the-money option will rise sharply while the theta of in-the-money and out-of-the-money options will drop.

THE GREEKS: SUMMARY

Forecasting the behavior of the price of an option before expiration is a complex proposition because there are multiple factors that go into the equation, and if any one of these factors changes, they all change. Remembering to think in terms of possible price outcomes at expiration can be helpful. Spread trading can be even more complex because there are long and short positions spread over multiple strikes. Chapter 5 is devoted to the examination of the Greeks of the long butterfly and long condor spreads.

CHAPTER 4 EXERCISE

1. At-the-money options will have the highest vega. True or false?
2. Delta measures the sensitivity of an option with respect to interest rates. True or false?
3. Long calls and puts can have both positive and negative deltas. True or false?
4. The more time until expiration, the more sensitive the delta of an option is to a change in the underlying price. True or false?
5. Long options positions have a positive gamma and short options positions have a negative gamma. True or false?
6. If the delta of a long call changes from 0.40 to 0.60, with a 1-point change in the underlying, it would have a gamma of 0.20. True or false?
7. At-the-money options have the highest gamma. True or false?
8. Long options positions have negative theta and short options positions have positive theta. True or false?
9. Delta can be viewed as the probability of an option expiring in-the-money. True or false?
10. Near-term options are more sensitive to changes in implied volatility than longer-term options. True or false?

CHAPTER 4 QUIZ

1. Assume the following: Buy one XYZ June 105 call with thirty days to expiration. XYZ is trading at 110. The delta of the call is 70. If XYZ moves from 110 to 111, how much does the call premium increase or decrease?

2. The absolute value of vega will be identical with call and put options having the same strike and expiration. True or false?

3. Long options positions have positive vega and short options positions have negative vega. True or false?

4. At-the-money puts have a delta of ____, and at-the-money calls have a delta of ____.

5. Name the six inputs used in the theoretical pricing model referred to in this chapter.

6. The absolute value of theta will be different with call and put options having the same strike and expiration. True or false?

7. Assume the following: XYZ is trading at 110. The delta of the put is –40. If XYZ moves from 110 to 109, by how much does the put premium increase or decrease?

8. The premium of a May 40 call with a theta of –0.30 will erode by $0.30 with one day in time passing. True or false?

9. Assume the following: The XYZ 65 call has a vega of 0.35. If the premium of the 65 call is $8.00 and volatility increases by 1 point, then what is the new option premium?

10. An option premium's extrinsic value will erode at the most rapid rate eighty days to expiration, sixty days to expiration, or ten days to expiration?

Chapter 4 Exercise Answer Key

1. True
2. False. Delta describes the sensitivity of an option's price with respect to changes in the option's underlying's price.
3. False. Calls have positive deltas, and puts have negative deltas.
4. False. The more time until expiration, the less sensitive the delta of an option is to changes in price.
5. True
6. True
7. True
8. True
9. True
10. False. Longer-dated options are more sensitive to changes in implied volatility, as a projected rise or fall of implied volatility over a longer period is extrapolated to a much larger (in the case of rising volatility) or much smaller (in the case of falling volatility) range of possible price outcomes at expiration.

Chapter 4 Quiz Answer Key

1. Increases by $0.70
2. True
3. True
4. –50, +50
5. Underlying price, strike price, time to expiration, interest rates, dividends, implied volatility.
6. False. The absolute value of the theta will be identical with call and put options of the same strike and expiration.
7. Increases by $0.40
8. True
9. $8.35
10. Ten days

5

Application of the Greeks

CONCEPT REVIEW

Delta. The sensitivity (rate of change) of an option's theoretical value (assessed value) to a $1 change in the price of the underlying instrument.

Gamma. The sensitivity (rate of change) of an option's delta with respect to a 1-point change in the underlying's price.

Theta. The sensitivity (rate of change) of theoretical option prices to changes in time. Theta measures the rate of decay in the time value of options.

Vega. The sensitivity (rate of change) of an option's theoretical value to a change in implied volatility.

Chapter 4 introduces the Greeks—the partial derivatives used to measure the sensitivity of an option's premium to changing conditions. Because long butterfly and condor spreads are made of combinations of long *and* short options, spread over three or more strikes, it is important to understand the Greeks of these particular structures.

Even though the Greeks of a position at a given moment in time are the sum of the Greeks of the component strikes, understanding how the Greeks of these strikes shift *in relation to each other* as conditions change is critical to understanding how the spread may behave. With spreads consisting of both long and short option positions, the sensitivities of long butterflies (or condors) can flip-flop depending on market conditions such as the option's underlying price, time to expiration, volatility levels, and so forth. It is also important to understand when, where, and why these changes occur in order to anticipate how the value of the spread will be affected as conditions change.

• **Author's Note**

Call butterflies (condors) and put butterflies (condors) are generally equivalent; therefore, for the sake of simplicity, in this book they are referred to generically as "butterflies (condors)" with the understanding that the term refers to both.

INTUITING THE GREEKS

Before running off for an options calculator or position analyzer, first try to use a little intuition when considering the Greeks of these structures. For example, we know that a long butterfly (condor) strategy is intended for a sideways market, where, it is hoped, the option's underlying's price ends up at a certain location (the middle strike, or, in the case of the condor, anywhere between the two middle strikes) at a certain time (expiration). Because we know where we would like the option's underlying to be, and when we would like it to be there, if we think about the strategy a bit we should be able to approximate the Greeks of the position without resorting to a calculator. This type of mental exercise can raise one's comfort level with the strategy and help avoid the dreaded "paralysis by analysis" syndrome that can afflict traders using position analyzers on basic strategies.

THE GREEKS

Delta

Delta may be used to measure the sensitivity of a position structure to changes in the underlying's price. The delta of a position structure is the sum of the deltas of the individual subcomponents. The theoretical point of maximum potential profit is when the underlying's price is at the middle strike (between the middle strikes for a condor) at expiration. If the underlying's price is below the middle strike(s), we want the underlying's price to rise, implying that the position will have a *long* delta. If the underlying's price is above the middle strike(s), we want the underlying's price to fall, implying that the position will have a *short* delta. Also, because the strategies have limited risk and limited return, at some point on the upper and lower extremes the delta returns to zero.

Unfortunately, determining delta is not quite that simple. Recall from Chapter 4 that there are other market conditions that may affect the delta of a structure. Even though it may be easy to understand that the delta of a long butterfly (condor) is *long* below the middle strike(s) and *short* above the middle strike(s), we need to consider *how long* and *how short*, as well as *how sensitive* the delta is in order to understand the price sensitivity of these position structures. **Figure 5.1** and **Figure 5.2** chart the delta of the long 95/100/105 butterfly and the long 90/95/100/105 condor at various underlying prices as expiration approaches.

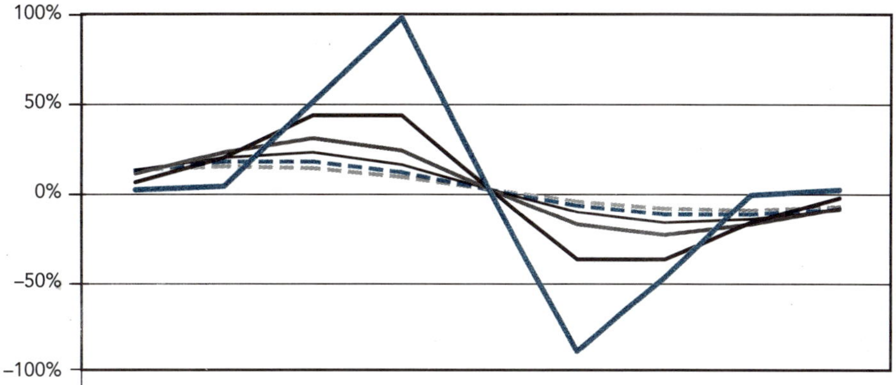

	90	92.5	95	97.5	100	102.5	105	107.5	110
0 days	0.00	0.02	0.50	0.98	–0.01	–0.92	–0.50	–0.03	0.00
2 days	0.04	0.18	0.42	0.42	0.00	–0.40	–0.40	–0.19	–0.05
4 days	0.09	0.21	0.29	0.22	0.00	–0.20	–0.26	–0.20	–0.11
6 days	0.11	0.18	0.21	0.14	0.00	–0.13	–0.19	–0.17	–0.12
8 days	0.11	0.16	0.16	0.10	0.00	–0.09	–0.14	–0.14	–0.11
10 days	0.11	0.13	0.12	0.07	0.00	–0.07	–0.11	–0.12	–0.10

Figure 5.1 Butterfly Delta vs. Price and Time *Source: Corona Derivatives, LLC*

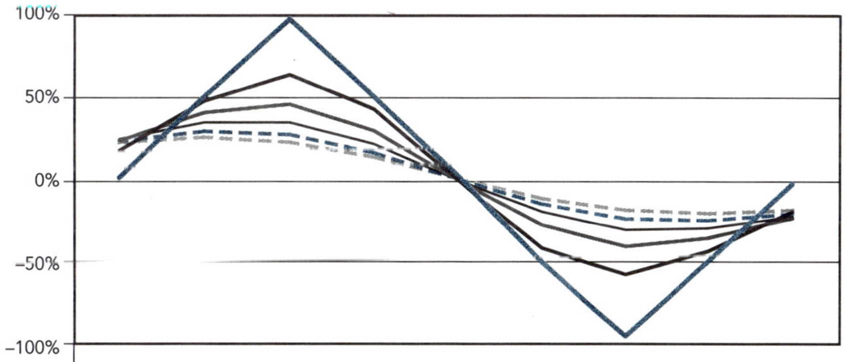

	87.5	90	92.5	95	97.5	100	102.5	105	107.5
0 days	0.01	0.50	0.97	0.50	0.02	–0.50	–0.95	–0.50	–0.03
2 days	0.17	0.47	0.63	0.42	–0.01	–0.42	–0.58	–0.44	–0.20
4 days	0.23	0.40	0.45	0.29	–0.01	–0.28	–0.41	–0.36	–0.24
6 days	0.24	0.34	0.34	0.21	–0.01	–0.20	–0.31	–0.30	–0.23
8 days	0.23	0.29	0.27	0.16	0.00	–0.15	–0.24	–0.25	–0.21
10 days	0.22	0.25	0.22	0.13	0.00	–0.12	–0.19	–0.21	–0.19

Figure 5.2 Condor Delta vs. Price and Time *Source: Corona Derivatives, LLC*

Compare the delta when the underlying's price is around the middle strike(s), when expiration is near to the delta, and when there is more time to expiration. Take a look at the table in Figure 5.1. With ten days until expiration, a move from 97.50 to 103 in the underlying's price changes the delta of the long butterfly only from 0.07 to –0.07. On expiration day, however, the same move in underlying price changes the delta of the long butterfly from 0.98 to –0.92. The delta of an at-the-money option increases dramatically as expiration approaches.

When the underlying's price is near the middle strike(s), the value of the butterfly (condor) becomes increasingly sensitive as expiration approaches. This makes sense intuitively because expiration day is when the final outcome is determined and extrinsic value vanishes. On expiration day, with the underlying slightly below the middle strike the position will approach 100 percent (long). If the underlying is slightly above the middle strike, the position will approach 100 percent (short).

Recall from Chapter 4 that in terms of impact on the Greeks, rising and falling implied volatility levels mimic time to expiration moving backward and forward. Rising implied volatility mimics time to expiration increasing; falling implied volatility mimics time to expiration decreasing. Notice the similarity between **Figure 5.3** and Figure 5.1.

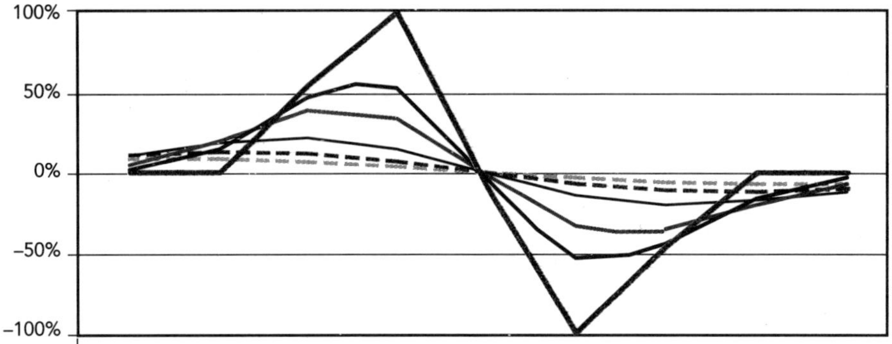

	90	92.5	95	97.5	100	102.5	105	107.5	110
5%	0.00	0.00	0.54	1.00	–0.08	–1.00	–0.46	0.00	0.00
15%	0.02	0.15	0.47	0.53	–0.03	–0.53	–0.44	–0.16	–0.03
20%	0.05	0.20	0.39	0.34	–0.01	–0.33	–0.35	–0.20	–0.07
30%	0.11	0.19	0.22	0.15	0.00	–0.14	–0.20	–0.17	–0.12
40%	0.11	0.13	0.12	0.07	0.00	–0.07	–0.11	–0.12	–0.10
50%	0.09	0.09	0.07	0.04	0.00	–0.03	–0.06	–0.07	–0.07

Figure 5.3 Butterfly Delta vs. Price and Volatility
Source: Corona Derivatives, LLC

Gamma

The sensitivity (rate of change) of the delta of an option to changes in the underlying's price is expressed by gamma. Recall the main points about gamma from Chapter 4:

- At-the-money options always have the highest gamma.
- Gamma of an at-the-money option rises sharply as expiration approaches.
- Gamma of in- and out-of-the-money options falls as expiration approaches.
- Long options have positive gamma.
- Short options have negative gamma.

These points are critical to understanding how the price sensitivity of a winged spread strategy such as a long butterfly or condor evolves over time. Because there are long and short options in different locations, the gamma of the position can take on different characteristics depending on the underlying's price. Also, with the short options grouped in the center of these structures, the negative gamma can become large if the underlying is in the vicinity of the short options and expiration is approaching (or if implied volatility is falling). **Figure 5.4** charts the gamma of the long 95/100/105 butterfly at various prices of the underlying as expiration approaches.

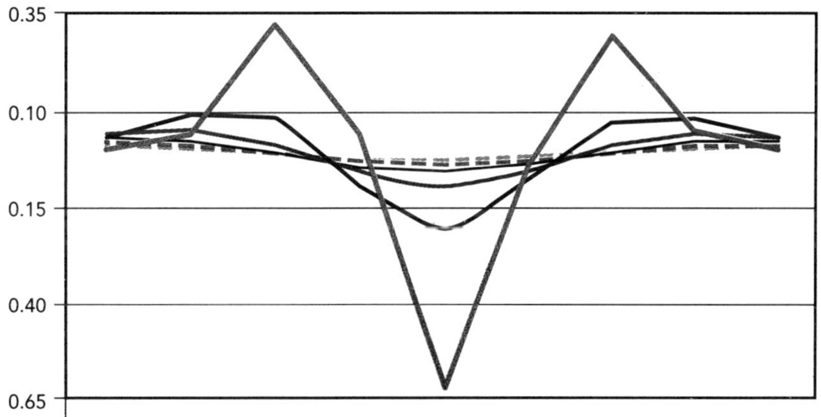

	90	92.5	95	97.5	100	102.5	105	107.5	110
0 days	0.00	0.04	0.33	0.04	–0.63	–0.04	0.30	0.05	0.00
2 days	0.03	0.09	0.08	–0.10	–0.20	–0.08	0.06	0.08	0.03
4 days	0.04	0.05	0.01	–0.06	–0.10	–0.06	0.01	0.04	0.03
6 days	0.03	0.02	–0.01	–0.05	–0.06	–0.04	–0.01	0.02	0.02
8 days	0.02	0.01	–0.01	–0.03	–0.04	–0.03	–0.01	0.01	0.01
10 days	0.01	0.00	–0.01	–0.03	–0.03	–0.02	–0.01	0.00	0.01

Figure 5.4 Butterfly Gamma vs. Price and Time
Source: Corona Derivatives, LLC

Notice, particularly in the shortest-dated options, how the gamma shifts as the underlying's price changes, moving from a long gamma exposure in the vicinity of the long wings to a short gamma exposure in the vicinity of the short body of the structure. This is what causes the violent delta shifts as the underlying's price passes over the middle strike(s) when expiration is near. Notice also how the graph softens moving back through time. The same gamma shifts, and, thus, delta shifts, are evident, but much less violent. Move back far enough in time and the structure throws off very little gamma regardless of where the underlying's price happens to be—meaning it loses much of its delta sensitivity, and thus its sensitivity to movement of the underlying's price.

Vega

Vega measures the sensitivity of an option's theoretical price to changes in implied volatility. Recall the main points about vega from Chapter 4:

- At-the-money options always have the highest vega.
- Longer-dated options have a greater vega than shorter-dated options.
- Long options have positive vega.
- Short options have negative vega.

It is also worthwhile to recall the relationship of the vega of at-the-money strikes with the vega of in-the-money and out-of-the-money strikes. As time passes, the vegas of all of the strikes decrease, but the in-the-money and out-of-the-money strikes fall off faster, as can be seen in **Figure 5.5**.

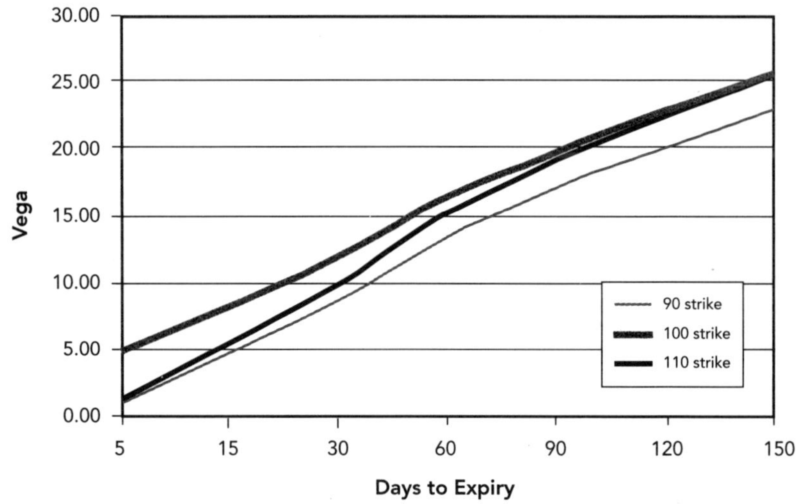

Figure 5.5 Vega vs. Time to Expiry [Stock Price = 100]
Source: Corona Derivatives, LLC

Because the relationship of the vegas of the different strikes remains tight until expiration approaches (or the base levels of implied volatility drop far enough), the impact of fluctuations in implied volatility on the price of a structure such as a long butterfly or condor is somewhat muted until expiration begins to approach (or base levels of implied volatility drop far enough). Essentially, the long butterfly (condor) "grows a vega" over time. **Figure 5.6** illustrates this.

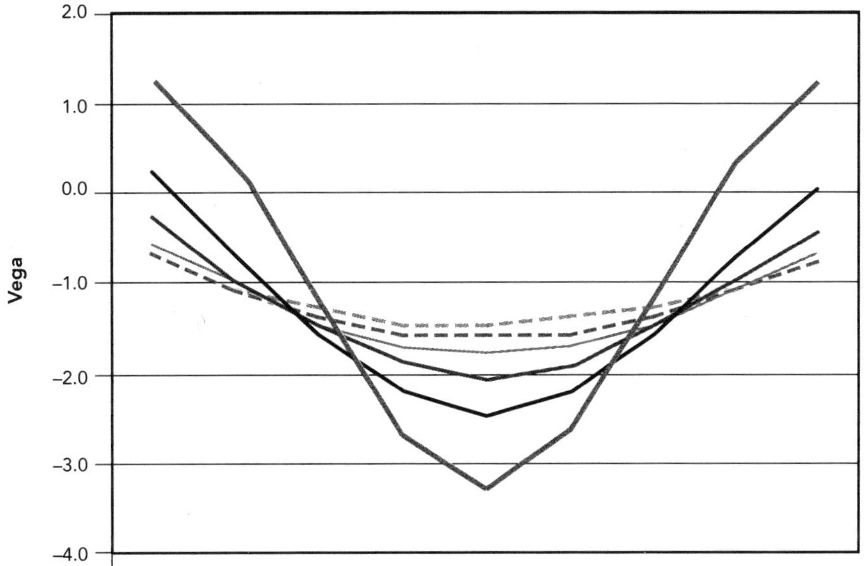

	90	92.5	95	97.5	100	102.5	105	107.5	110
10 days	1.3	0.0	–1.2	–2.7	–3.3	–2.6	–1.2	0.3	1.2
20 days	0.2	–0.7	–1.6	–2.2	–2.5	–2.2	–1.6	–0.7	0.1
30 days	–0.3	–1.0	–1.5	–1.9	–2.1	–1.9	–1.5	–1.0	–0.4
40 days	–0.6	–1.0	–1.5	–1.7	–1.8	1.7	–1.5	–1.1	–0.7
50 days	–0.7	–1.1	–1.4	–1.6	–1.6	–1.6	–1.4	–1.1	–0.8
60 days	–0.7	–1.1	–1.3	–1.5	–1.5	–1.4	–1.3	–1.1	–0.8

Figure 5.6 Butterfly Vega vs. Time *Source: Corona Derivatives, LLC*

Notice that with sixty days until expiration, the vega of the long butterfly (condor) is slightly negative, but fairly uniform across a broad range of underlying prices. With a long time to expiration, changes in implied volatility do not have a drastic impact on the value of the butterfly. However, as time moves forward, the vegas of the in-the-money and out-of-the-money options begin to drop off at a faster rate than the at-the-money options, and the vega of the long butterfly (condor) structure becomes increasingly negative when the underlying's price is near the short middle strike(s), where it is more sensitive to changes in implied volatility.

Also notice that, as the underlying's price moves to the extremes, the vega of the structure flips to positive. Changes in the base levels of implied volatility also mimic these characteristics. **Figure 5.7** charts the relationship between the vega of a long butterfly and base levels of implied volatility.

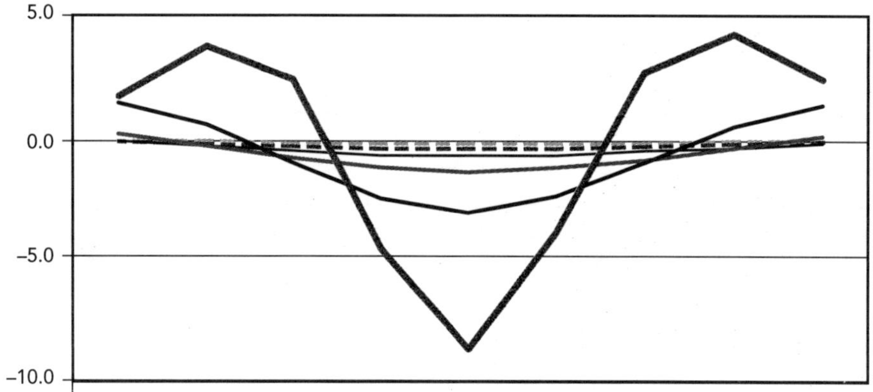

	90	92.5	95	97.5	100	102.5	105	107.5	110
20%	1.6	3.7	2.3	–4.8	–9.0	–4.1	2.6	4.2	2.3
40%	0.3	0.4	–1.2	–2.7	–3.3	–2.6	–1.2	0.3	1.2
60%	0.0	–0.5	–1.0	–1.4	–1.6	–1.4	–1.1	–0.6	–0.1
80%	–0.3	–0.5	–0.7	–0.9	–0.9	–0.9	–0.7	–0.6	–0.4
100%	–0.3	–0.4	–0.5	–0.6	–0.6	–0.6	–0.5	–0.4	–0.3
120%	–0.3	–0.3	–0.4	–0.4	–0.4	–0.4	–0.4	–0.3	–0.3

Figure 5.7 Butterfly Vega vs. Implied Volatility
Source: Corona Derivatives, LLC

Once again, changes in implied volatility levels can mimic time. Notice that at 100 percent implied volatility the vega of the long butterfly (condor) is slightly negative but uniform across a broad range of underlying prices. At high base levels of implied volatility, changes in implied volatility do not have a drastic impact on the value of the spread. However, as base levels of implied volatility decline and the vega of the in-the-money and out-of-the-money options begins to drop off faster than the at-the-money options, the vega of the long butterfly (condor) structure becomes increasingly negative when the underlying's price is near the short middle strike(s), becoming more sensitive to changes in implied volatility. Notice also that as the underlying's price moves to the extremes, the vega of the structure flips to positive.

Theta

Theta measures the sensitivity of an option's theoretical price to the passage of time. Recall the main points about theta from Chapter 4:

- At-the-money options always have the highest theta.
- Theta of an at-the-money option rises sharply as expiration approaches.
- Thetas of in- and out-of-the-money options fall as expiration approaches.
- Long options have negative theta.
- Short options have positive theta.

Time decay is the key to a winged spread strategy such as a long butterfly (condor), and the key to time decay in any spread position is *location*. Prior to expiration, if the long butterfly (condor) is properly located so that the short options constituting the body of the structure are at or near the underlying's price, the structure will have positive time decay. As time passes, the rate of decay will accelerate as the theta of the at-the-money options rises while the theta of the in-the-money and out-of-the-money options falls. This causes the theta of the long butterfly (condor) structure to rise sharply when the underlying's price is at or near the middle strike(s). **Figure 5.8** charts the theta of a long butterfly at various prices of the underlying as expiration approaches.

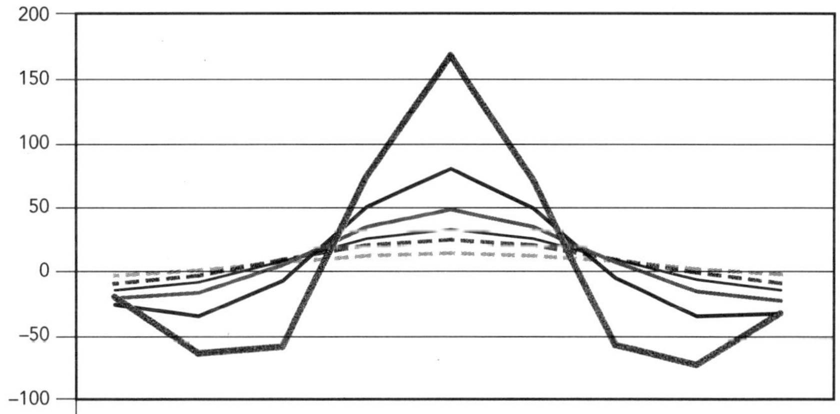

	90	92.5	95	97.5	100	102.5	105	107.5	110
2 days	−19	−62	−57	72	164	70	−56	−71	−32
4 days	−25	−34	−7	49	78	48	−5	−34	−32
6 days	−20	−16	5	34	47	34	7	−15	−22
8 days	−14	−8	8	25	32	25	9	−6	−14
10 days	−9	−3	9	20	24	20	9	−1	−9
15 days	−3	1	7	12	14	12	8	2	−2

Figure 5.8 Butterfly Theta vs. Days to Expiry
Source: Corona Derivatives, LLC

This chart should be getting familiar by now. Note how the theta rises sharply (becomes increasingly positive) when the underlying's price is near the middle strike(s) and time to expiration is passing. Also note the importance of location, how the theta shifts as the underlying's price changes, moving from a positive theta exposure in the vicinity of the short body of the structure to a negative theta exposure out on the wings. Notice also that moving back through time, the same theta shifts occur, but are softer. Move back far enough in time and the structure throws off very little theta regardless of where the underlying's price happens to be—meaning it loses much of its sensitivity to the passage of time.

SUMMARY

The long butterfly (condor) is a "target trade," targeting a certain location (the middle strike or between the middle strikes) at a certain time (expiration). When there is considerable time remaining until expiration, in other words, plenty of *time* left to hit the target, it is not particularly sensitive to changes in market conditions; it is usually a stable structure. It will have a negligible delta, gamma, vega, and theta. Of course, the same is true when the base level of implied volatility is very high—that is, plenty of projected *movement* left to hit the target, and may exhibit similar stability, having the same negligible delta, gamma, vega, and theta. Under these conditions, the gamma, theta, and vegas of the component strikes involved are very similar to one another, and because there are equal amounts of long and short options in the structure, the exposures largely offset one another, lowering the sensitivity of the structure to market changes.

These relationships unravel when time to expiration begins to pass, or base levels of implied volatility begin to fall. The derivative exposure of the strikes involved start to evolve, becoming quite different from one another, and the structure becomes quite sensitive to changing market conditions, taking on the characteristics of short options when the underlying's price is at or near the middle strike(s)—short gamma, short vega, positive theta—or reversing to take on the characteristics of long options when the underlying's price is near the outer strikes—long gamma, long vega, negative theta.

Knowing and understanding how the sensitivity of these position structures evolves is the key to managing these types of positions.

CHAPTER 5 EXERCISE

1. Consider the 50/55/60 long call butterfly. If the underlying security's price is just above the 55 strike, is this a long or short delta position?

2. With the underlying security trading at 71 and three days until expiration, does the delta of the 65/70/75 long put butterfly become more sensitive or less sensitive as expiration approaches?

3. Consider the 100/105/110 long call butterfly. The underlying is trading at 100. The position has a positive delta. The best-case scenario would be for the underlying to be at 105 at expiration. True or false?

4. Consider the 30/35/40/45 long call condor. The 30 and 35 strikes have a positive gamma, and the 40 and 45 strikes have a negative gamma. True or false?

5. Consider the 20/30/40 long put butterfly. The underlying is trading at 40. Which strike has the highest gamma?

6. Consider the 30/40/45/50 long call condor. The farther out from expiration, are the delta and gamma more sensitive or less sensitive?

7. Consider the 30/35/40 long put butterfly. The 30 and 40 strikes have positive vega, and the 35 has negative vega. True or false?

8. Consider the 30/35/40/45 long call condor. As expiration approaches, do the vegas of all four strikes increase or decrease?

9. Consider the 50/60/70 long put butterfly. The underlying is trading at 59. Which strike would have the highest theta?

10. Consider a long call butterfly. It has a negative theta exposure outside of the lowest and highest strikes. True or false?

CHAPTER 5 QUIZ

1. Consider the 90/100/105 long call butterfly. The underlying is trading at 90. If the market moves from 90 to 112, the delta for this position would then be negative. True or false?

2. With the underlying trading at 100, and three days until expiration, which butterfly will have the greatest delta sensitivity?

   a. 95/100/105

   b. 90/95/100

   c. 100/105/110

3. Consider the 80/85/90 long call butterfly. The underlying is trading at 80. As expiration approaches, the gamma of the 80 options rises sharply and the gamma of the 85 and 90 options falls sharply. True or false?

4. Within several days of expiration, the underlying price changes and the position moves from a short gamma exposure in the area of the wings to a long gamma exposure in the area of the body. True or false?

5. As expiration approaches, the in-the-money and out-of-the-money option vegas decrease at a faster rate than the at-the-money options. True or false?

6. As expiration approaches, does the vega of the long condor become increasingly positive or increasingly negative with the underlying's price near the middle strikes?

7. Consider the 20/25/30/35 long condor. The underlying is trading at 20. As expiration approaches, the theta of the 20 strike rises more sharply than the thetas of the 25, 30, and 35 strikes. True or false?

8. Consider the 30/35/40/45 long put condor. The underlying is trading at 35. Do the 30 and 45 strikes have positive or negative thetas?

9. As time passes, the rate of decay will accelerate as the thetas of the at-the-money options rise. True or false?

10. Consider the 30/35/40 long call butterfly. As the underlying's price changes, the theta moves from positive in the area of the body to negative in the wings. True or false?

Chapter 5 Exercise Answer Key

1. Short
2. More sensitive
3. True
4. False. The 30 and 45 have positive gamma, and the 35 and 40 have negative gamma.
5. 40
6. Less sensitive
7. True
8. Decrease
9. 60
10. True

Chapter 5 Quiz Answer Key

1. True
2. a.
3. True
4. False. Within several days of expiration, the underlying price changes and the position moves from a long gamma exposure in the area of the wings to a short gamma exposure in the area of the body.
5. True
6. Increasingly negative
7. True
8. Negative thetas
9. True
10. True

6

Understanding Iron Butterflies and Condors

CONCEPT REVIEW

Box spread. An option spread that involves a long call and a short put at one strike price and a short call and a long put at another strike price, all in the same expiration month.

Bull spread. A strategy that includes two or more options series of the same type that may profit from a rise in the underlying's price. It also can be a strategy that involves an option contract(s) and an underlying position.

Bear spread. A strategy that includes two or more option series of the same type that may profit from a decline in the underlying's price. It also can be a strategy that involves an option contract(s) and an underlying position.

Credit spread. A spread in which the difference between the long and short options premiums results in a net credit. Two examples would be a put bull spread and a call bear spread.

Carrying cost. The amount of interest expense on money borrowed to finance a position.

Debit spread. A spread in which the difference between the long and short options premiums results in a net debit. Two examples would be a put bear spread and a call bull spread.

Synthetic. Two or more trading vehicles (call, put, underlying) packaged together to emulate another trading vehicle or spread. Some examples include:

(long call = long put + long underlying) (short call = short put + short underlying)

(long put = long call + short underlying) (short put = short call + long underlying)

(long underlying = long call + short put) (short underlying = short call + long put)

Vertical spread. A spread that involves the simultaneous purchase and sale of options of the same class at different strike prices but with the same expiration date.

One structure that has grown in popularity recently is the "iron" butterfly (condor). This structure is a synthetic version of a long call or put butterfly (condor) and is composed entirely of out-of-the-money options. Because of the way it is structured, the long iron butterfly (condor) will result in a credit to the buyer—one reason for its popularity—and because it is composed entirely of out-of-the-money options it has less execution risk if the end user decides to execute it in stages—a second reason for its popularity. However, it is important that the end user understand the relationship between the iron butterfly (condor) and the call or put butterfly (condor) in order to discern its special characteristics.

COMPARING LONG CALL AND PUT BUTTERFLIES AND LONG CALL AND PUT CONDORS

Chapters 2 and 3 explore the structure and P&L diagrams of long butterflies and condors composed of either all calls or all puts. One of the interesting characteristics of the structures is that long call and put butterflies and long call and put condors are a combination of two vertical spreads (a bull spread and a bear spread). In the case of the long butterfly, a bull spread at the lower two strikes is *overlapped by* a bear spread at the upper two strikes. (See **Figure 6.1**.) In the case of the long condor, a bull spread at the lower two strikes is *adjacent to* a bear spread at the upper two strikes. (See **Figure 6.2**.)

Bull Call Spread K_1,K_2	+	Bear Call Spread K_2,K_3	=	Long Call Butterfly K_1,K_2,K_3	Strike
+1				+1	K_1
–1		–1		–2	K_2
		+1		+1	K_3
Bull Put Spread K_1,K_2	**+**	**Bear Put Spread K_2,K_3**	**=**	**Long Put Butterfly K_1,K_2,K_3**	**Strike**
+1				+1	K_1
–1		–1		–2	K_2
		+1		+1	K_3

Figure 6.1 Overlapping Bull and Bear Spreads Form Long Call and Put Butterflies *Source: Corona Derivatives, LLC*

Bull Call Spread K_1,K_2	+	Bear Call Spread K_3,K_4	=	Long Call Condor	Strike
+1				+1	K_1
–1				–1	K_2
		–1		–1	K_3
		+1		+1	K_4
Bull Put Spread K_1,K_2	**+**	**Bear Put Spread K_3,K_4**	**=**	**Long Put Condor**	**Strike**
+1				+1	K_1
–1				–1	K_2
		–1		–1	K_3
		+1		+1	K_4

Figure 6.2 Adjacent Bull and Bear Spreads Form Long Call and Put Condors *Source: Corona Derivatives, LLC*

After examining the P&L diagrams and examples of the long call and put butterflies in Chapter 2, and the long call and put condors in Chapter 3, it is clear that the risk/reward profiles of these structures are *generally* identical.[1] The reason for this relationship is that the component bull and bear vertical spreads that make up a long butterfly or a long condor happen to be synthetically equivalent to one another (same strikes, same expiration), as shown in **Figure 6.3** and **Figure 6.4**.

1. There are exceptions. Situations with the possibility of early exercise of American-style options can cause put and call butterflies, and put and call condors, to have different pricing.

Bull Call Spread K_1,K_2	=	Bull Put Spread K_1,K_2
+1	K_1	+1
–1	K_2	–1
(Debit Spread)		(Credit Spread)

Figure 6.3 Bull Call Spread = Bull Put Spread
Source: Corona Derivatives, LLC

Bear Call Spread K_3,K_4	=	Bear Put Spread K_3, K_4
–1	K_3	–1
+1	K_4	+1
(Credit Spread)		(Debit Spread)

Figure 6.4 Bear Call Spread = Bear Put Spread
Source: Corona Derivatives, LLC

SINCE:

Bull Call Spread K_1,K_2	=	Bull Put Spread K_1, K_2
+1	K_1	+1
–1	K_2	–1
(Debit Spread)		(Credit Spread)

AND:

Bear Call Spread K_2,K_3	=	Bear Put Spread K_2, K_3
–1	K_2	–1
+1	K_3	+1
(Credit Spread)		(Debit Spread)

THEN:

Long Call Butterfly K_1,K_2,K_3	=	Long Put Butterfly K_1,K_2,K_3
+1	K_1	+1
–2	K_2	–2
+1	K_3	+1

Figure 6.5 Long Call Butterfly = Long Put Butterfly
Source: Corona Derivatives, LLC

Because the component structures are synthetically equivalent, the long butterfly or condor structures comprising these components must also be synthetically equivalent. This is shown in **Figure 6.5** and **Figure 6.6**.

SINCE:		
Bull Call Spread K_1,K_2	=	Bull Put Spread K_1,K_2
+1	K_1	+1
–1	K_2	–1
(Debit Spread)		(Credit Spread)
AND:		
Bear Call Spread K_3,K_4	=	Bear Put Spread K_3,K_4
–1	K_3	–1
+1	K_4	+1
(Credit Spread)		(Debit Spread)
THEN:		
Long Call Condor K_1,K_2,K_3,K_4	=	Long Put Condor K_1,K_2,K_3,K_4
+1	K_1	+1
–1	K_2	–1
–1	K_3	–1
+1	K_4	+1

Figure 6.6 Long Call Condor = Long Put Condor
Source: Corona Derivatives, LLC

GUTS

Because call bull spreads are synthetically equal to put bull spreads and call bear spreads are synthetically equal to put bear spreads, we also should be able to construct long butterfly or condor positions with any combination of lower strike bull vertical and upper strike bear vertical spreads. The combinations in **Figure 6.7** and **Figure 6.8** yield two new permutations of the long butterfly: the long "guts" iron butterfly and the "classic" long iron butterfly.

Guts are similar to "strangles" in that they consist of the purchase (or sale) of both a put and a call at different strikes on the same underlying asset with the same expiration. The guts iron butterfly is long both the in-the-money call and the in-the-money put, or, in other words, it is composed of two debit spreads. However, unlike strangles, guts consist of both a lower strike call and a higher strike put. The guts will therefore have some intrinsic value at expiration, whereas the strangle could potentially finish worthless. The guts' value at expiration comes from either the call or put finishing in-the-money, or a combination of both the call and put finishing in-the-money.

Even though the guts iron butterfly is synthetically equivalent to other butterflies, it is not a vehicle recommended for the novice investor or trader. Because it contains two in-the-money legs that will generally have a wide bid-ask spread, it can be difficult to execute and riskier when "legging" in or out of the position. This spread is the domain of market makers and other market professionals. For these reasons we will ignore the guts iron butterfly (condor) in our discussions and instead focus on the classic iron butterfly.

Bull Call Spread K_1,K_2	+	Bear Put Spread K_2,K_3
+1	K_1	
–1	K_2	–1
	K_3	+1
(Debit Spread)		(Debit Spread)

EQUALS:

Long Guts Iron Butterfly

+1	K_1	
–1	K_2	–1
	K_3	+1

Figure 6.7 Long Guts Iron Butterfly *Source: Corona Derivatives, LLC*

Bear Call Spread K_2,K_3	+	Bull Put Spread K_1,K_2
	K_1	+1
–1	K_2	–1
+1	K_3	
(Credit Spread)		(Credit Spread)

EQUALS:

Classic Long Iron Butterfly

	K_1	+1
–1	K_2	–1
+1	K_3	

Figure 6.8 Classic Long Iron Butterfly *Source: Corona Derivatives, LLC*

Figure 6.9 and **Figure 6.10** illustrate the long guts iron condor and the classic long iron condor. Note that these permutations share the same characteristics of the ordinary long call and put butterflies and condors. They are composed of bull spreads at the lower strikes overlapping (adjacent to) bear spreads at the upper strikes. They also have the classic "long the wings and short the body" structure (+1/–2/+1 for the butterfly, or +1/–1/–1/+1 for the condor).

Bull Call Spread K_1,K_2	+	Bear Put Spread K_3,K_4
+1	K_1	
–1	K_2	
	K_3	–1
	K_4	+1
(Debit Spread)		(Debit Spread)

EQUALS:

	Long Guts Iron Condor	
+1	K_1	
–1	K_2	
	K_3	–1
	K_4	+1

Figure 6.9 Long Guts Iron Condor *Source: Corona Derivatives, LLC*

Bear Call Spread K_3,K_4	+	Bull Put Spread K_1,K_2
	K_1	+1
	K_2	–1
–1	K_3	
+1	K_4	
(Credit Spread)		(Credit Spread)

EQUALS:

	Classic Long Iron Condor	
	K_1	+1
	K_2	–1
–1	K_3	
+1	K_4	

Figure 6.10 Classic Long Iron Condor *Source: Corona Derivatives, LLC*

THE CLASSIC LONG IRON BUTTERFLY

The classic long iron butterfly is composed of two credit spreads: a bull put spread and a bear call spread. With credit spreads all the rage in the options world, this is a very popular spread. After all, why *pay* for a long call butterfly or a long put butterfly when you can construct a synthetically equivalent position for a *credit*, right? Wrong.

Pricing Anomalies

It would seem to make sense that a particular spread executed for a credit would be superior to a synthetically equivalent spread executed for a debit; after all, one can collect interest on a credit balance, whereas one must pay interest on a debit balance. Unfortunately, it is a bit more complicated than that, and the fact of the matter is that this advantage is usually a mirage.

There are no free lunches in options trading—there are not even free crumbs. Pricing models build interest costs, no matter how trivial, into the price of each option. This means that options prices are discounted to compensate for the cost of financing the position. The buyer of an option or a spread will pay slightly less premium to compensate for the fact that he will incur financing costs for his debit balance, whereas the seller of an option or a spread will receive slightly less premium to compensate for the fact that he will receive interest on his credit balance. This discounting tends to remove any advantage associated with a "credit vs. debit" trade of synthetically equivalent positions.

The Box

The best way to illustrate this pricing anomaly is to break out the interest-rate component that accounts for the difference in pricing between a long iron butterfly (condor) and a long call or put butterfly (condor). The structure that contains the interest-rate component and links the long call butterfly (condor), the long put butterfly (condor),

Bull Call Spread K_1,K_2	+	Bear Put Spread K_1,K_2
+1	K_1	–1
–1	K_2	+1
(Debit Spread)		(Debit Spread)
EQUALS:		
	Long Box Spread	
+1	K_1	–1
–1	K_2	+1

Figure 6.11 The Long Box Spread *Source: Corona Derivatives, LLC*

and the iron butterfly (condor) is a structure called a "box." A box is composed of a bull spread and a bear spread with the same strikes and same expiration. **Figure 6.11** and **Figure 6.12** illustrate the structure of a box spread.

Bear Call Spread K_1,K_2	+	Bull Put Spread K_1,K_2
−1	K_1	+1
+1	K_2	−1
(Credit Spread)		(Credit Spread)
EQUALS:		
	Short Box Spread	
−1	K_1	+1
+1	K_2	−1

Figure 6.12 The Short Box Spread *Source: Corona Derivatives, LLC*

Combining two debit spreads, a bull call spread, and a bear put spread (same strikes, same expiration) creates a long box spread. Combining two credit spreads, a bear call spread, and a bull put spread (same strikes, same expiration) creates a short box spread.

- **Box Value**

The box is a neutral structure with an interest-rate component. It has no delta, no gamma, no theta, no vega—it can't because it is composed of offsetting positions in two synthetically equivalent spreads (bull spread + bear spread = neutral). It does, however, have the interest-rate component, and it is this component that explains the difference in pricing between an iron butterfly and a regular butterfly. At expiration, the value of a box spread will always be the difference between its strike prices ($K_2 - K_1$); this is the "maturity value" of the box. Anytime before expiration it will trade at a discount to compensate for carrying costs. The discounted value or the "present value" of the difference between the strike prices yields the fair value of the box spread:

$$\text{BOX} = \frac{(K_2 - K_1)}{(1 + r)^t}$$

Where:
K_2 = Upper strike
K_1 = Lower strike
r = Interest rate, in decimal form
t = Time, in years

For example, what is the fair value of the 95/100 box spread with ninety days until expiration at an interest rate of 4.04 percent?

$$BOX = \frac{(100 - 95)}{(1 + .0404)^{(90/360)}} = \$4.95$$

This means that the present value of the box spread carries a 0.05 discount to the maturity value, to compensate for carrying costs. Now we will apply this to the relationship between a long call butterfly and a classic long iron butterfly to explain pricing differences, as shown in **Figure 6.13**.

Long Call Butterfly and Short Box Spread

Calls		Strike	Puts
+1	**–1**	**95**	**+1**
–2	**+1**	**100**	**–1**
+1		**105**	

EQUALS:

Classic Long Iron Butterfly

Calls	Strike	Puts
	95	**+1**
–1	**100**	**–1**
+1	**105**	

Figure 6.13 Long Call Butterfly and Classic Long Iron Butterfly Comparison *Source: Corona Derivatives, LLC*

From Figure 6.13 we can see that a long 95/100/105 call butterfly combined with a short 95/100 box results in a long 95/100/105 iron butterfly. Suppose the call butterfly were trading for $1.00. At what price should the iron butterfly be trading?

Long 95/100/105 Call Butterfly (debit) + Short 95/100 Box (credit)
= Iron Butterfly (credit)
= –1.00 + 4.95
= 3.95

Based on a box price of \$4.95, the long 95/100/105 call butterfly at a \$1.00 debit is synthetically equivalent to the long 95/100/105 iron butterfly at a \$3.95 credit. The P&L diagram in **Figure 6.14** illustrates the risk, reward, and break-even points of the classic iron butterfly at expiration.

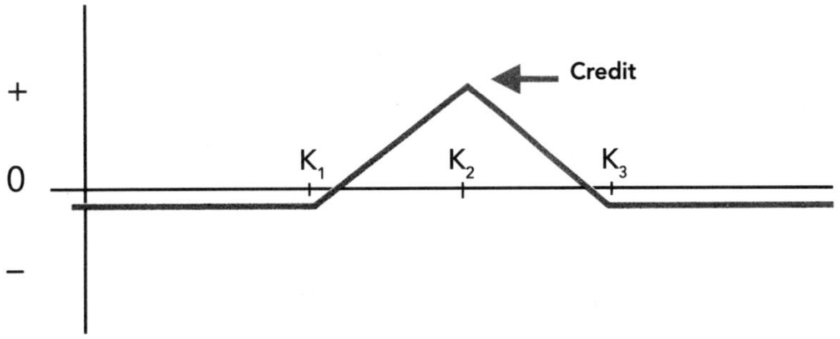

Composition:	Long 1 K_1 put Short 1 K_2 call; short 1 K_2 put Long 1 K_3 call Same expiry, same underlying
Max Profit:	Credit
Max Loss:	$(K_3 - K_1)/2$ – credit
Breakevens:	K_1 + max loss; K_3 – max loss

Figure 6.14 Long Iron Butterfly *Source: Corona Derivatives, LLC*

Example

Buy the XYZ April 95/100/105 Iron Butterfly:

- Buy 1 XYZ April 95 put at \$0.50
- Sell 1 XYZ April 100 call at \$3.00
- Sell 1 XYZ April 100 put at \$2.00
- Buy 1 XYZ April 105 call at \$0.55

This creates a long XYZ April 95/100/105 iron butterfly at a credit of \$3.95, as shown in **Figure 6.15** on the following page.

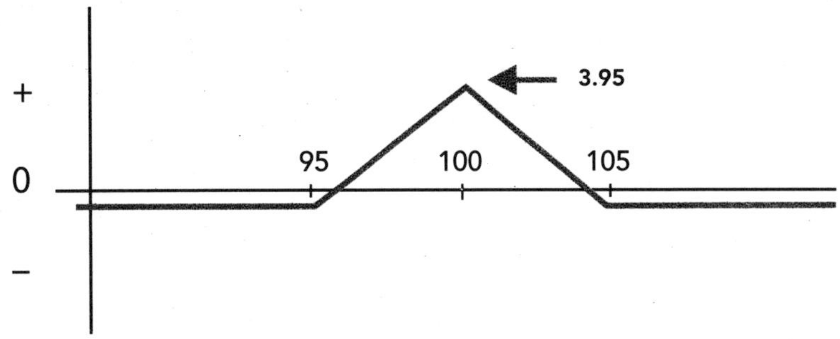

Composition:	Long 1 95 put Short 1 100 call; short 1 100 put Long 1 105 call Same expiry, same underlying
Max Profit:	3.95
Max Loss:	(105 – 95)/2 – 3.95 = 1.05
Breakevens:	96.05; 103.95

Figure 6.15 Long Iron Butterfly With Prices *Source: Corona Derivatives, LLC*

THE INTEREST IMPACT

So, if a long iron butterfly at a $3.95 credit is synthetically equivalent to a long call or put butterfly at a $1.00 debit, why do the payout values appear to differ? Why does the risk appear to be $1.00 for the long call or put butterfly but $1.05 for the long iron butterfly? Why does the reward appear to be $4.00 for the long call or put butterfly but $3.95 for the long iron butterfly?

The answer is in the interest rate costs, which are rarely addressed in traditional hockey-stick-type payout diagrams. If we adjust the two strategies for interest income/expense using 4 percent with ninety days until expiration:

- Long Call or Put Butterfly interest expense = 1.00 × 0.04 × 90/360 = 0.01
- Long Iron Butterfly interest income = 3.95 × 0.04 × 90/360 = 0.04

So, over the course of the trade, the long call or put butterfly will incur an interest expense of 0.01, while the long iron butterfly will generate interest income of 0.04. If the trades are adjusted by these amounts, the risk, reward, and break-even levels are exactly equal.

TRADING THE IRON BUTTERFLY

After wading through the last couple of pages it would be understandable if one never wanted to trade an iron butterfly (condor) again. Fear not! The iron butterfly (condor) has a lot going for it. It can be a great trading vehicle. Chapter 7 is devoted to long butterfly (condor) trading tactics, and many of these tactics revolve around the long iron butterfly and condor. Below are some of the characteristics of this structure that can make the iron butterfly a great trading vehicle:

- Out-of-the-money options—better liquidity (think pennies)
- Tighter bid-ask spreads, less legging risk
- Half bull spread, half bear spread
- Long strangle, short straddle
- Subcomponents can be added or subtracted as market view evolves

SUMMARY

All butterflies and condors are composed of either overlapping or adjacent bull and bear vertical spreads. Long butterflies are composed of a bull vertical spread at the lower two strikes *overlapped* by a bear vertical spread at the upper two strikes. Long condors are composed of a bull vertical spread at the lower two strikes adjacent to a bear vertical spread at the upper two strikes.

These bull and bear vertical spreads may be all call vertical spreads, all put vertical spreads, or they may be a mixture of call vertical spreads and put vertical spreads. When long butterflies and condors are composed of a mixture of call vertical spreads and put vertical spreads, they are known as long *iron* butterflies and condors.

Structure

Long iron butterflies and condors may take two forms: the long "guts" iron butterfly or condor or the long "classic" iron butterfly or condor.

The long "guts" iron butterfly is one in which the bull vertical spread at the lower strikes is a bull call spread and the overlapping bear vertical spread at the upper strikes is a bear put spread. The long "guts" iron condor is one in which the bull vertical spread at the lower strikes is a bull call spread and the adjacent bear vertical spread at the upper strikes is a bear put spread.

The long "classic" iron butterfly is one in which the bull vertical spread at the lower strikes is a bull put spread and the overlapping bear vertical spread at the upper strikes is a bear call spread. The long "classic" iron condor is one in which the bull vertical spread at the lower strikes is a bull put spread and the adjacent bear vertical spread at the upper strikes is a bear call spread.

Pricing

Because bull and bear call and put verticals of the same strikes and same expirations are synthetically equivalent, there is no difference between the risk, reward, or break-even points of a long call butterfly, a long put butterfly, a long "guts" iron butterfly, or a long "classic" iron butterfly (or condor). The difference in pricing between a long call or put butterfly or condor (generally executed for a debit), a long "guts" iron butterfly or condor (generally executed for a large debit), and a long "classic" iron butterfly or condor (generally executed for a credit), is the presence of a position called the "box." The box is a neutral position: a bull spread and a bear spread of the same strikes and expiration with an interest-rate component. Much like a Treasury bill, the box trades at a discount to maturity value throughout its life and will mature at a value equal to $K_2 - K_1$. The long "guts" iron butterfly has a long box embedded in the position, causing the large debit, while the long "classic" iron butterfly has a short box embedded in the position, causing the credit. After the effect of the box position is removed, all butterflies and condors of the same strikes and expirations are equal.

The Iron Butterfly As a Trading Vehicle

Because the long "classic" iron butterfly is composed entirely of out-of-the-money options, it may provide an excellent trading vehicle. Out-of-the-money options generally have a tighter bid-ask spread, lower deltas (and therefore less execution risk), and greater liquidity, which may make it easier, less costly, and less risky getting into and out of long "classic" iron butterfly or condor positions.

CHAPTER 6 EXERCISE

1. The long call butterfly is trading at \$2.00, interest rate is 5 percent, and there are ninety days until expiration. Calculate the interest expense for the long call butterfly.

2. The long guts iron butterfly is long the at-the-money call and the at-the-money put. True or false?

3. Construct a classic long iron butterfly, given the following strikes. Indicate whether you are buying or selling each contract.

C	K	P
	80	
	85	
	90	

4. A put bull spread and a put bear spread = a long put butterfly or a long call butterfly spread?

5. Construct a long call butterfly given the following strikes. Indicate whether you are buying or selling each contract.

C	K	P
	60	
	65	
	70	

6. A long butterfly spread can be viewed as a ______ spread at the lower two strikes, overlapped by a __________ spread at the upper two strikes.

7. Because a call bull spread equals a put bull spread and a call bear spread equals a put bear spread, a long call condor equals a long put condor. True or false?

8. What strategy is this structure?

   Long 1 call at the 45 strike
   Short 1 call at the 50 strike
   Short 1 call at the 55 strike
   Long 1 call at the 60 strike

9. Construct a long 90/100 box.

C	K	P
	90	
	100	

10. Construct a short 60/65 box.

C	K	P
	60	
	65	

CHAPTER 6 QUIZ

1. A long box spread can be viewed as a long call vertical and a long put vertical. True or false?
2. An example of a short box spread would be short the Aug 60/70 call spread and long the Aug 60/70 put spread. True or false?
3. At expiration, a box spread should always be worth exactly the difference between the strikes. True or false?
4. A long call butterfly (or a long put butterfly) can be viewed as a combination of two ____________________ spreads.
5. A long condor is a <u>*bull/bear*</u> spread at the <u>*upper/lower*</u> two strikes, adjacent to a <u>*bull/bear*</u> spread at the <u>*upper/lower*</u> two strikes.
6. Bull call spreads are synthetically equivalent to ____ _____ spreads.
7. The composition of a long guts iron butterfly is two debit spreads. True or false?
8. What is the composition of the long guts iron condor?
9. Is the classic long iron butterfly composed of two debit or two credit spreads?
10. If you purchased both the 65/70/75 put butterfly and the 60/65/70 put butterfly, what would be the resulting position?

Chapter 6 Exercise Answer Key

1. 0.025 ($2.00 × 0.05 × 90/360)
2. False (long the in-the-money call and put)
3.

C	K	P
	80	+1
–1	85	–1
+1	90	

4. Long put butterfly
5.

C	K	P
+1	60	
–2	65	
+1	70	

6. Bull; bear
7. True
8. Long call condor
9.

C	K	P
+1	90	– 1
–1	100	+1

10.

C	K	P
–1	60	+1
+1	65	–1

Chapter 6 Quiz Answer Key

1. True
2. False (short both the call and put spreads)
3. True
4. Vertical
5. Bull, lower; bear, upper
6. Bull put
7. True
8.

C	K	P
+1	K_1	
–1	K_2	
	K_3	–1
	K_4	+1

9. Credit
10. Long the 60/65/70/75 put condor

7

Popular Mutant Structures:

Broken-Wing Butterflies, Pterodactyls, and Iron Pterodactyls

CONCEPT REVIEW

Broken-wing butterfly. Similar to a standard butterfly; however, the outer strikes are not equidistant from the inner strikes.

Pterodactyl. The pterodactyl is a long condor with a gap between the middle strikes. It retains the bull spread at the lower strikes, bear spread at the upper strikes composition. The distance between the wing strikes and the body strikes is equal, giving it a symmetrical P&L diagram.

Iron pterodactyl. An iron pterodactyl is simply a regular pterodactyl with a synthetically equivalent credit spread substituted for the debit spread portion of the position.

One of the biggest difficulties faced by the beginning option trader is keeping up with the terminology. Many of the phrases were created on the spot years ago by professional traders, and logical or not, they persist today ("Jelly-roll," anyone?). In addition, the recent explosion in the popularity of options trading as a result of electronic access and lower costs has helped create a second wave of terminology.

As the options industry has grown, so too have related businesses such as those offering options education, data, trading advice, tools, trading platforms, and so on. Various types of education, including books and other written material, online and live seminars, intensive training courses, "boot camps," and the like, are readily available to the options consumer. Indeed, options trading infomercials are giving real estate seminars, therapeutic beds, exercise equipment, and juicers a run for their money on late-night television.

Many of the educational websites offer exciting "new" strategies and attach exotic names to them, creating additional confusion for the beginner. However, most of these new strategies are traditional strategies with embedded sub-strategies—usually designed to generate additional premium "credits." This chapter dissects and analyzes some of the more popular misnomers.

THE BROKEN-WING BUTTERFLY

As noted in Chapter 2, a winged structure such as a long butterfly or condor has strikes that are equidistant between the wings and body. This gives the structure the symmetrical P&L properties readers should be familiar with by now. When the strikes are not equidistant, the structure will have an asymmetrical P&L. This asymmetry is generated by an embedded vertical spread, creating a type of structure popularly referred to as a *broken-wing butterfly*. A broken-wing butterfly is really two positions combined: a butterfly and a vertical spread (a credit spread), as indicated in **Figure 7.1** and **Figure 7.2**. Because both the long butterfly and the vertical spread (credit spread) are limited risk/limited reward structures, the broken-wing butterfly is also a limited risk/limited reward structure. It shares this characteristic with the plain-vanilla butterfly—however, the similarities end there.

Long Broken-Wing Call Butterfly

Long Call Butterfly K_1,K_2,K_3	+	Short Call Spread K_3,K_4	=	Broken-Wing Call Butterfly K_1,K_2,K_4	Strike
+1				+1	K_1
–2				–2	K_2
+1		–1			K_3
		+1		+1	K_4

Figure 7.1 Structure of the Long Broken-Wing Call Butterfly
Source: Corona Derivatives, LLC

Strike	Long Put Butterfly K_2,K_3,K_4	+	Short Put Spread K_1,K_2	=	Broken-Wing Put Butterfly K_1,K_3,K_4
K_1			+1		+1
K_2	+1		–1		
K_3	–2				–2
K_4	+1				+1

Figure 7.2 Structure of the Long Broken-Wing Put Butterfly
Source: Corona Derivatives, LLC

The strikes selected for a broken-wing butterfly can vary, with the trader choosing a less aggressive or more aggressive credit spread to tailor the risk/reward profile according to his market view. This has the effect of lowering risk on one side of the spread and raising risk on the other. A long broken-wing call butterfly has the embedded credit spread *above* the body, and a long broken-wing put butterfly has the embedded credit spread *below* the body. **Figure 7.3** illustrates the payout diagram of a long broken-wing call butterfly.

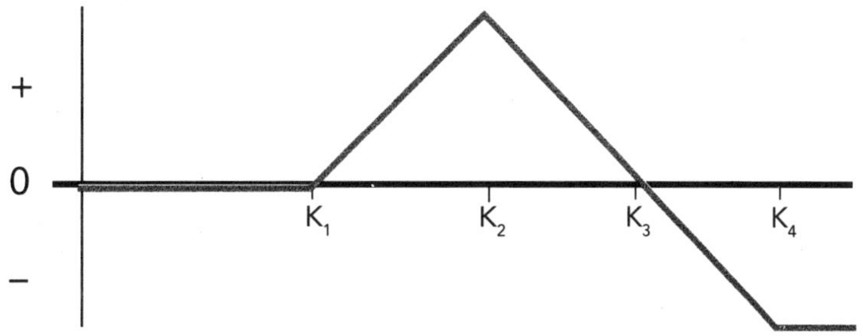

Composition:	Long 1 K_1 call
	Short 2 K_2 calls
	Long 1 K_4 call
	Same expiry, same underlying
Max Upside Profit:	$(K_2 - K_1)$ +(–) credit (debit)
Max Downside Profit:	Credit (if any)
Max Downside Loss:	Debit (if any)
Max Upside Loss:	$(K_4 - K_3)$ –(+) credit (debit)
Breakevens:	
Downside	K_1 + debit (if any)
Upside	K_3 (–)+ (debit) credit

Figure 7.3 Long Broken-Wing Call Butterfly P&L Diagram
Source: Corona Derivatives, LLC

Obviously the risk/reward and break-even points of this structure are a little messy, because this type of structure has an asymmetrical P&L profile. Both upside and downside risks and break-even points have to be calculated separately. Also, depending on market conditions, the spread could possibly be executed for a debit *or* a credit, a nuance which also needs to factored in to the equation.

Example

Buy the XYZ April 95/100/110 Broken-Wing Call Butterfly:

- Buy 1 XYZ April 95 call at $7.00
- Sell 2 XYZ April 100 calls at $4.00
- Buy 1 XYZ April 110 call at $0.50

This creates a long XYZ April 95/100/110 broken-wing call butterfly at a credit of $0.50, as shown in **Figure 7.4**.

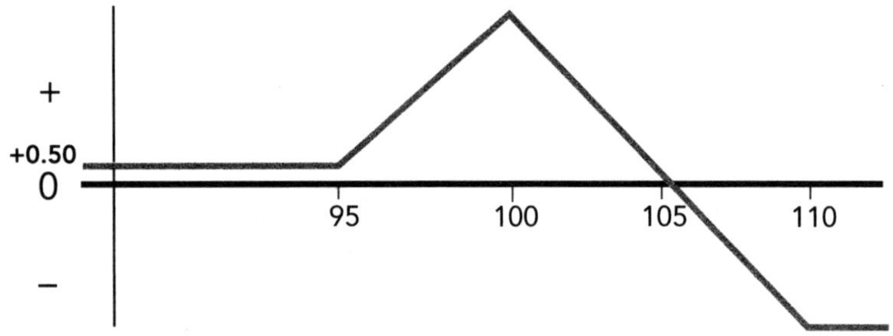

Composition:	Long 1 95 call
	Short 2 100 calls
	Long 1 110 call
	Same expiry, same underlying
Max Upside Profit:	(100 – 95) + 0.50 = 5.50
Max Downside Profit:	0.50
Max Downside Loss:	N/A
Max Upside Loss:	(110 – 105) – 0.50 = 4.50
Breakevens:	
Downside	N/A
Upside	105 + 0.50 = 105.50

Figure 7.4 P&L Diagram of the Long XYZ 95/100/110 Broken-Wing Call Butterfly *Source: Corona Derivatives, LLC*

"What If?" Scenarios (Potential Outcomes at Expiration)

Stock Price of 90.00	Long 1 XYZ April 95 call value	=	$0.00
	Short 2 XYZ April 100 calls value	=	$0.00
	Long 1 XYZ April 110 call value	=	$0.00
	Net value of spread	=	$0.00
	Cost of spread (credit)	=	$0.50
	Net profit/loss	**=**	**$0.50**
Stock Price of 95.00	Long 1 XYZ April 95 call value	=	$0.00
	Short 2 XYZ April 100 calls value	=	$0.00
	Long 1 XYZ April 110 call value	=	$0.00
	Net value of spread	=	$0.00
	Cost of spread (credit)	=	$0.50
	Net profit/loss	**=**	**$0.50**

Stock Price of 100.00	Long 1 XYZ April 95 call value	=	$5.00
	Short 2 XYZ April 100 calls value	=	$0.00
	Long 1 XYZ April 110 call value	=	$0.00
	Net value of spread	=	$5.00
	Cost of spread (credit)	=	$0.50
	Net profit/loss	**=**	**$5.50**
Stock Price of 105.50	Long 1 XYZ April 95 call value	=	$10.50
	Short 2 XYZ April 100 calls value	=	–$11.00
	Long 1 XYZ April 110 call value	=	$0.00
	Net value of spread	=	–$0.50
	Cost of spread (credit)	=	$0.50
	Net profit/loss	**=**	**$0.00**
Stock Price of 110.00	Long 1 XYZ April 95 call value	=	$15.00
	Short 2 XYZ April 100 calls value	=	–$20.00
	Long 1 XYZ April 110 call value	=	$0.00
	Net value of spread	=	–$5.00
	Cost of spread (credit)	=	$0.50
	Net profit/loss	**=**	**–$4.50**

Long Broken-Wing Put Butterfly

The long broken-wing put butterfly has its embedded credit spread below the body. **Figure 7.5** illustrates the payout diagram of a long broken-wing put butterfly.

Again, because this type of structure has an asymmetrical P&L diagram, upside and downside risks as well as break-even points have to be calculated separately. Also, depending on market conditions, the spread could possibly be executed for a debit *or* a credit, a nuance which also needs to be factored in to the equation.

Example

Buy the XYZ April 95/105/110 Broken-Wing Put Butterfly:

- Buy 1 XYZ April 95 put at $0.50
- Sell 2 XYZ April 105 puts at $4.50
- Buy 1 XYZ April 110 put at $9.00

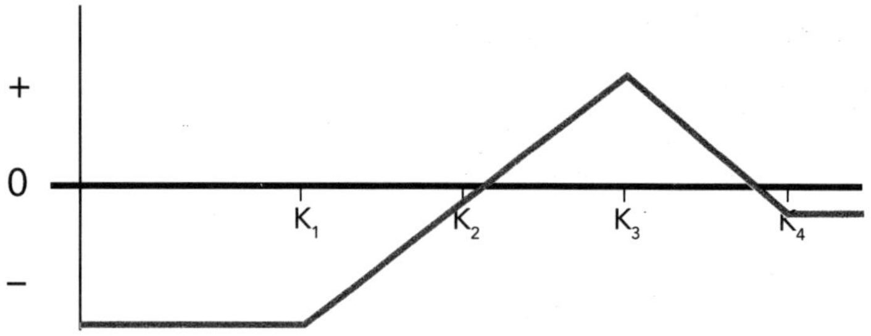

Composition: Long 1 K_1 put
Short 2 K_3 puts
Long 1 K_4 put
Same expiry, same underlying
Max Upside Profit: Credit (if any)
Max Downside Profit: $(K_4 - K_3)$ +(–) credit (debit)
Max Downside Loss: $(K_2 - K_1)$ –(+) credit (debit)
Max Upside Loss: Debit (if any)
Breakevens:
Downside K_2 (+)– (debit) credit
Upside K_4 – debit (if any)

Figure 7.5 Long Broken-Wing Put Butterfly P&L Diagram
Source: Corona Derivatives, LLC

This creates a long XYZ April 95/100/110 broken-wing put butterfly at a total cost of $0.50, as shown in **Figure 7.6**.

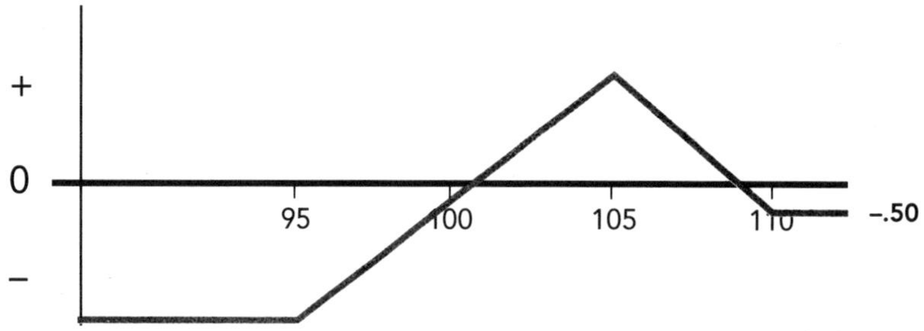

Composition: Long 1 95 put
Short 2 105 puts
Long 1 110 put
Same expiry, same underlying
Max Upside Profit: N/A
Max Downside Profit: (110 – 105) – 0.50 = 4.50
Max Downside Loss: (100 – 95) + 0.50 = 5.50
Max Upside Loss: 0.50
Breakevens:
Downside 100 + 0.50 = 100.50
Upside 110 – 0.50 = 109.50

Figure 7.6 P&L Diagram of the Long XYZ 95/105/110 Broken-Wing Put Butterfly *Source: Corona Derivatives, LLC*

"What If?" Scenarios (Potential Outcomes at Expiration)

Stock Price of 95.00	Long 1 XYZ April 95 put value	=	$0.00
	Short 2 XYZ April 105 puts value	=	–$20.00
	Long 1 XYZ April 110 put value	=	$15.00
	Net value of spread	=	–$5.00
	Cost of spread	=	$0.50
	Net profit/loss	**=**	**–$5.50**
Stock Price of 100.50	Long 1 XYZ April 95 put value	=	$0.00
	Short 2 XYZ April 105 puts value	=	–$9.00
	Long 1 XYZ April 110 put value	=	$9.50
	Net value of spread	=	$0.50
	Cost of spread	=	$0.50
	Net profit/loss	**=**	**$0.00**
Stock Price of 105.00	Long 1 XYZ April 95 put value	=	$0.00
	Short 2 XYZ April 105 puts value	=	$0.00
	Long 1 XYZ April 110 put value	=	$5.00
	Net value of spread	=	$5.00
	Cost of spread	=	$0.50
	Net profit/loss	**=**	**$4.50**
Stock Price of 109.50	Long 1 XYZ April 95 put value	=	$0.00
	Short 2 XYZ April 105 puts value	=	$0.00
	Long 1 XYZ April 110 put value	=	$0.50
	Net value of spread	=	$0.50
	Cost of spread	=	$0.50
	Net profit/loss	**=**	**$0.00**
Stock Price of 115.00	Long 1 XYZ April 95 put value	=	$0.00
	Short 2 XYZ April 105 puts value	=	$0.00
	Long 1 XYZ April 110 put value	=	$0.00
	Net value of spread	=	$0.00
	Cost of spread	=	$0.50
	Net profit/loss	**=**	**–$0.50**

An examination of the payout diagrams and the what-if examples shows that there are some similarities between the broken-wing butterfly and the regular butterfly. For example, both achieve potential maximum profitability at the short strike (the body) *at expiration*. However, the long broken-wing call butterfly takes its potential maximum loss at or above the *upper* strike, while the long put broken-wing butterfly takes its potential maximum loss at or below the *lower* strike.

THE BROKEN-WING CONDOR

The previous examples were of broken-wing butterflies, although they could just as easily have been condors. Embed a credit spread into the position so that the wing strikes are not equidistant from the body strikes, and presto! You have a broken-wing condor. (See **Figure 7.7**.)

Long Broken-Wing Call Condor

Long Call Condor K_1, K_2, K_3, K_4	+	Short Call Spread K_4, K_5	=	Broken-Wing Call Condor K_1, K_2, K_3, K_5	Strike
+1				+1	**K_1**
–1				–1	**K_2**
–1				–1	**K_3**
+1		–1			**K_4**
		+1		+1	**K_5**

Figure 7.7 Structure of the Long Broken-Wing Call Condor
Source: Corona Derivatives, LLC

The strike selection process for the broken-wing condor is the same as the broken-wing butterfly, with the credit spread chosen for embedding into the original condor structure determined by the trader's market view, and the credit spread being embedded above the body of the structure. **Figure 7.8** illustrates the payout diagram of a long broken-wing call condor.

Because of the involvement of even more strikes, the risk/reward of the long broken-wing call condor is even messier than that of the long broken-wing call butterfly. Once again, because it is a structure with an asymmetrical P&L profile, the upside and downside risks and break-even points need to be calculated separately. Also, depending on market conditions, the spread possibly could be executed for a debit or a credit, a nuance which needs to be factored into the equation.

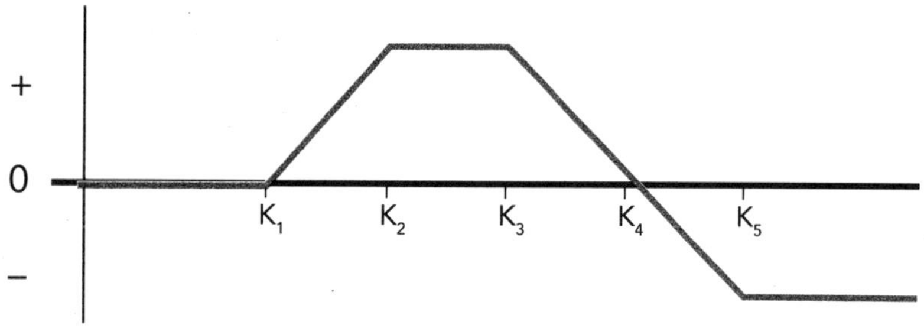

Composition:	Long 1 K_1 call Short 1 K_2 call Short 1 K_3 call Long 1 K_5 call Same expiry, same underlying
Max Upside Profit:	$(K_2 - K_1)$ +(–) credit (debit)
Max Downside Profit:	Credit (if any)
Max Downside Loss:	Debit (if any)
Max Upside Loss:	$(K_5 - K_4)$ –(+) credit (debit)
Breakevens:	
Downside	K_1 + debit (if any)
Upside	K_4 (–)+ (debit) credit

Figure 7.8 Long Broken-Wing Call Condor P&L Diagram
Source: Corona Derivatives, LLC

Example

Buy the XYZ April 95/100/105/115 Broken-Wing Call Condor:

- Buy 1 XYZ April 95 call at $7.00
- Sell 1 XYZ April 100 call at $4.00
- Sell 1 XYZ April 105 call at $2.00
- Buy 1 XYZ April 115 call at $0.10

This creates a long XYZ April 95/100/105/115 broken-wing call condor at a debit of $1.10 as shown in **Figure 7.9**.

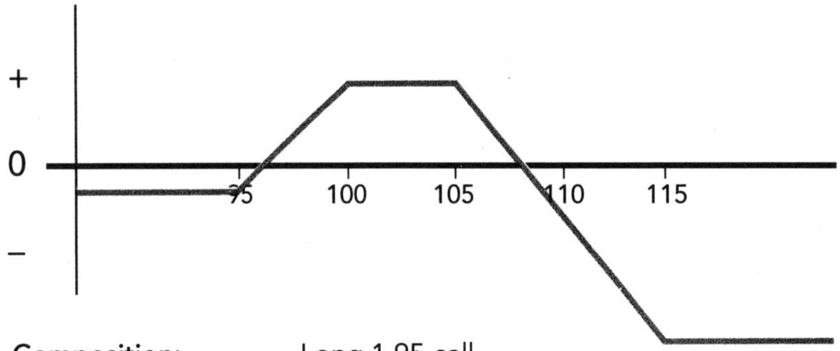

Composition: Long 1 95 call
Short 1 100 call
Short 1 105 call
Long 1 115 call
Same expiry, same underlying

Max Upside Profit: (100 – 95) – 1.10 = 3.90
Max Downside Profit: NA
Max Downside Loss: 1.10
Max Upside Loss: (115 –110) + 1.10 = 6.10
Breakevens:
Downside 95 + 1.10 = 96.10
Upside 110 – 1.10 = 108.90

Figure 7.9 Diagram of the Long XYZ April 95/100/105/115 Broken-Wing Call Condor *Source: Corona Derivatives, LLC*

"What If?" Scenarios (Potential Outcomes at Expiration)

Stock Price of 95.00	Long 1 XYZ April 95 call value	=	$0.00
	Short 1 XYZ April 100 call value	=	$0.00
	Short 1 XYZ April 105 call value	=	$0.00
	Long 1 XYZ April 115 call value	=	$0.00
	Net value of spread	=	$0.00
	Cost of spread	=	$1.10
	Net profit/loss	**=**	**–$1.10**
Stock Price of 96.10	Long 1 XYZ April 95 call value	=	$1.10
	Short 1 XYZ April 100 call value	=	$0.00
	Short 1 XYZ April 105 call value	=	$0.00
	Long 1 XYZ April 115 call value	=	$0.00
	Net value of spread	=	$1.10
	Cost of spread	=	$1.10
	Net profit/loss	**=**	**$0.00**

Stock Price of 100.00	Long 1 XYZ April 95 call value	=	$5.00
	Short 1 XYZ April 100 call value	=	$0.00
	Short 1 XYZ April 105 call value	=	$0.00
	Long 1 XYZ April 115 call value	=	$0.00
	Net value of spread	=	$5.00
	Cost of spread	=	$1.10
	Net profit/loss	**=**	**$3.90**
Stock Price of 105.00	Long 1 XYZ April 95 call value	=	$10.00
	Short 1 XYZ April 100 call value	=	–$5.00
	Short 1 XYZ April 105 call value	=	$0.00
	Long 1 XYZ April 115 call value	=	$0.00
	Net value of spread	=	$5.00
	Cost of spread	=	$1.10
	Net profit/loss	**=**	**$3.90**
Stock Price of 108.90	Long 1 XYZ April 95 call value	=	$13.90
	Short 1 XYZ April 100 call value	=	–$8.90
	Short 1 XYZ April 105 call value	=	–$3.90
	Long 1 XYZ April 115 call value	=	$0.00
	Net value of spread	=	$1.10
	Cost of spread	=	$1.10
	Net profit/loss	**=**	**$0.00**
Stock Price of 115.00	Long 1 XYZ April 95 call value	=	$20.00
	Short 1 XYZ April 100 call value	=	–$15.00
	Short 1 XYZ April 105 call value	=	–$10.00
	Long 1 XYZ April 115 call value	=	$0.00
	Net value of spread	=	–$5.00
	Cost of spread	=	$1.10
	Net profit/loss	**=**	**–$6.10**

Long Broken-Wing Put Condor

Strike	Long Put Condor K_2,K_3,K_4,K_5	+	Short Put Spread K_1,K_2	=	Broken-Wing Put Condor K_1,K_3,K_4,K_5
K_1			+1		+1
K_2	+1		–1		
K_3	–1				–1
K_4	–1				–1
K_5	+1				+1

Figure 7.10 Structure of the Long Broken-Wing Put Condor
Source: Corona Derivatives, LLC

Like the broken-wing put butterfly, the broken-wing put condor has its embedded credit spread below the body of the structure, lowering the risk to the upside, but raising it to the downside, and the credit spread chosen for the embedding depends on the trader's market view and risk appetite. **Figure 7.11** illustrates the payout diagram of a long broken-wing put condor:

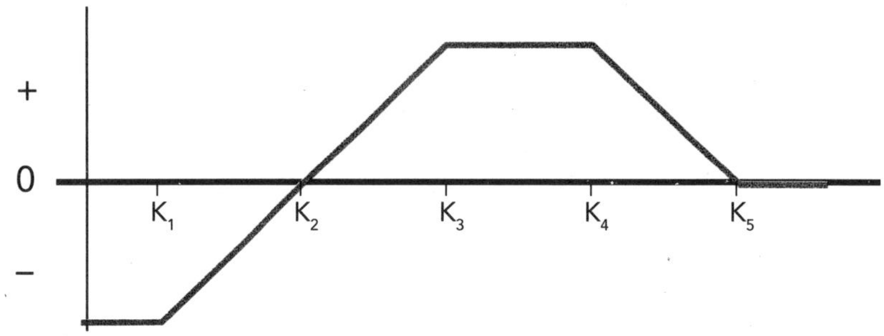

Composition:	Long 1 K_1 put Short 1 K_3 put Short 1 K_4 put Long 1 K_5 put Same expiry, same underlying
Max Upside Profit:	Credit (if any)
Max Downside Profit:	$(K_5 - K_4)$ +(–) credit (debit)
Max Downside Loss:	$(K_2 - K_1)$ –(+) credit (debit)
Max Upside Loss:	Debit (if any)
Breakevens:	
Downside	K_2 (+)– (debit) credit
Upside	K_5 – debit (if any)

Figure 7.11 Long Broken-Wing Put Condor P&L Diagram
Source: Corona Derivatives, LLC

Example

Buy the XYZ April 95/105/110/115 Broken-Wing Put Condor:

- Buy 1 XYZ April 95 put at $0.50
- Sell 1 XYZ April 105 put at $3.00
- Sell 1 XYZ April 110 put at $6.00
- Buy 1 XYZ April 115 put at $ 9.50

This creates a long XYZ April 95/105/105/115 broken-wing call condor at a debit of $1.00 as shown in **Figure 7.12**.

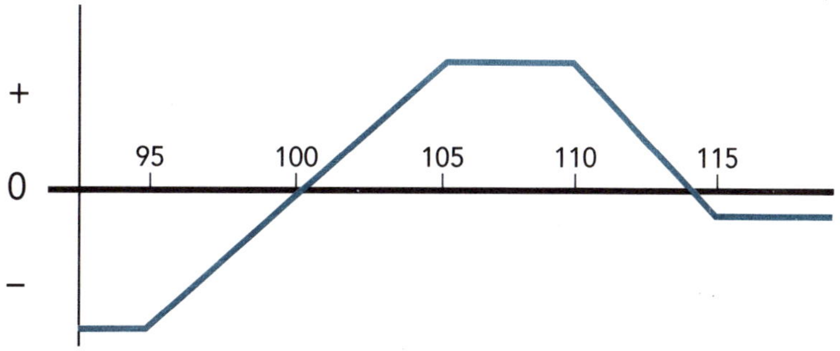

Composition:	Long 1 95 put Short 1 105 put Short 1 110 put Long 1 115 put Same expiry, same underlying
Max Upside Profit:	NA
Max DownsideProfit:	(115 – 110) – 1.00 = 4.00
Max Downside Loss:	(100 – 95) + 1.00 = 6.00
Max Upside Loss:	1.00
Breakevens:	
Downside	100 + 1.00 = 101.00
Upside	115 – 1.00 = 114.00

Figure 7.12 Diagram of the Long XYZ 95/105/110/115 Broken-Wing Put Condor *Source: Corona Derivatives, LLC*

"What If?" Scenarios (Potential Outcomes at Expiration)

Stock Price of 95.00	Long 1 XYZ April 95 put value	=	$0.00
	Short 1 XYZ April 105 put value	=	–$10.00
	Short 1 XYZ April 110 put value	=	–$15.00
	Long 1 XYZ April 115 put value	=	$20.00
	Net value of spread	=	–$5.00
	Cost of spread	=	$1.00
	Net profit/loss	**=**	**–$6.00**
Stock Price of 101.00	Long 1 XYZ April 95 put value	=	$0.00
	Short 1 XYZ April 105 put value	=	–$4.00
	Short 1 XYZ April 110 put value	=	–$9.00
	Long 1 XYZ April 115 put value	=	$14.00
	Net value of spread	=	$1.00
	Cost of spread	=	$1.00
	Net profit/loss	**=**	**$0.00**
Stock Price of 105.00	Long 1 XYZ April 95 put value	=	$0.00
	Short 1 XYZ April 105 put value	=	$0.00
	Short 1 XYZ April 110 put value	=	–$5.00
	Long 1 XYZ April 115 put value	=	$10.00
	Net value of spread	=	$5.00
	Cost of spread	=	$1.00
	Net profit/loss	**=**	**$4.00**
Stock Price of 110.00	Long 1 XYZ April 95 put value	=	$0.00
	Short 1 XYZ April 105 put value	=	$0.00
	Short 1 XYZ April 110 put value	=	$0.00
	Long 1 XYZ April 115 put value	=	$5.00
	Net value of spread	=	$5.00
	Cost of spread	=	$1.00
	Net profit/loss	**=**	**$4.00**
Stock Price of 114.00	Long 1 XYZ April 95 put value	=	$0.00
	Short 1 XYZ April 105 put value	=	$0.00
	Short 1 XYZ April 110 put value	=	$0.00

	Long 1 XYZ April 115 put value	=	$1.00
	Net value of spread	=	$1.00
	Cost of spread	=	$1.00
	Net profit/loss	**=**	**$0.00**
Stock Price of 115.00	Long 1 XYZ April 95 put value	=	$0.00
	Short 1 XYZ April 105 put value	=	$0.00
	Short 1 XYZ April 110 put value	=	$0.00
	Long 1 XYZ April 115 put value	=	$0.00
	Net value of spread	=	$0.00
	Cost of spread	=	$1.00
	Net profit/loss	**=**	**–$1.00**

MOTIVATIONS BEHIND THE TRADE

The broken-wing butterfly or condor is not usually placed at-the-money; it usually has a directional bias. A long broken-wing call butterfly (condor) usually has a bullish bias and is placed above the underlying's price, so that the underlying has to move up through the area of potential maximum profitability *first*, before testing the area of potential maximum loss. A specific market view of "up, slowly" is needed to justify this trade. Of course, the extra credit generated softens the loss if one is wrong and the market falls.

Conversely, the long broken-wing put butterfly (condor) usually has a bearish bias, and is placed below the underlying's price, so that the underlying has to move down through the area of potential maximum profitability first, before testing the area of potential maximum loss. A specific market view of "down, slowly" is needed to justify this trade, and again, the extra credit generated softens the loss if one is wrong and the market rises.

PTERODACTYLS (IRON AND OTHERWISE)

Continuing with larger winged structures, we have the *pterodactyl* (sometimes referred to as the *albatross*). Both the pterodactyl and the broken-wing butterfly are variations of the same trade, and their "iron" synthetic equivalents are currently quite popular. Recall from Chapter 3 that two overlapping butterflies form a condor. (See **Figure 7.13**.)

If we carry this idea to extremes, it evolves into the "pterodactyl," as shown in **Figure 7.14** on page 112.

Long Call Condor

Call Butterfly K_1,K_2,K_3	+	Call Butterfly K_2,K_3,K_4	=	Call Condor K_1,K_2,K_3,K_4	Strike
+1				+1	K_1
–2		+1		–1	K_2
+1		–2		–1	K_3
		+1		+1	K_4

Long Put Condor

Put Butterfly K_1,K_2,K_3	+	Put Butterfly K_2,K_3,K_4	=	Put Condor K_1,K_2,K_3,K_4	Strike
+1				+1	K_1
–2		+1		–1	K_2
+1		–2		–1	K_3
		+1		+1	K_4

Figure 7.13 Comparison of the Long Call Condor and Long Put Condor Structure *Source: Corona Derivatives, LLC*

Long Call Pterodactyl

Call Butterfly K_1,K_2,K_3	+	Call Butterfly K_2,K_3,K_4	+	Call Butterfly K_3,K_4,K_5	=	Call Pterodactyl K_1,K_2,K_3,K_4,K_5	Strike
+1						+1	K_1
–2		+1				–1	K_2
+1		–2		+1			K_3
		+1		–2		–1	K_4
				+1		+1	K_5

Long Put Pterodactyl

Put Butterfly K_1,K_2,K_3	+	Put Butterfly K_2,K_3,K_4	+	Put Butterfly K_3,K_4,K_5	=	Put Pterodactyl K_1,K_2,K_3,K_4,K_5	Strike
+1						+1	K_1
–2		+1				–1	K_2
+1		–2		+1			K_3
		+1		–2		–1	K_4
				+1		+1	K_5

Figure 7.14 Comparison of the Long Call Pterodactyl and Long Put Pterodactyl Structure *Source: Corona Derivatives, LLC*

The pterodactyl is a long condor with a gap between the middle strikes. It retains the "bull spread at the lower strikes, bear spread at the upper strikes" characteristics of all long winged structures, and the distance between the wing strikes and the body strikes is equal, giving it a symmetrical payout, as seen in **Figure 7.15** below. Obviously, by continuing to overlap the position with long butterflies, we could create a long pterodactyl with a very large gap between the two short strikes, and this could conceivably carry on until strikes ran out. By constructing a position like this, the trader is essentially buying a larger area of potential maximum profitability. However, the additional money invested lowers the potential maximum return and raises the risk should the underlying's price move outside the wing strikes.

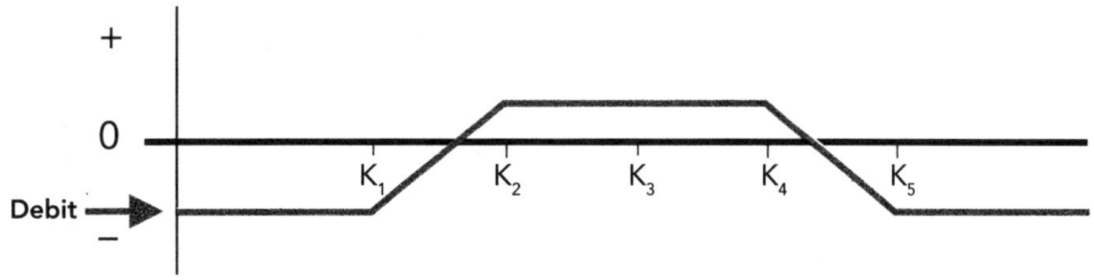

Composition:	Long 1 K_1 call Short 1 K_2 call Short 1 K_4 call Long 1 K_5 call Same expiry, same underlying
Max Profit:	$(K_2 - K_1)$ – debit
Max Loss:	Debit
Breakevens:	K_1 + debit; K_5 – debit

Figure 7.15 Long Call Pterodactyl P&L Diagram
Source: Corona Derivatives, LLC

Example

Buy the XYZ 95/100/110/115 Call Pterodactyl:

- Buy 1 XYZ April 95 call at $7.00
- Sell 1 XYZ April 100 call at $4.00
- Sell 1 XYZ April 110 call at $1.00
- Buy 1 XYZ April 115 call at $0.10

This creates a long XYZ April 95/100/110/115 call pterodactyl at a debit of $2.10, as shown in **Figure 7.16**.

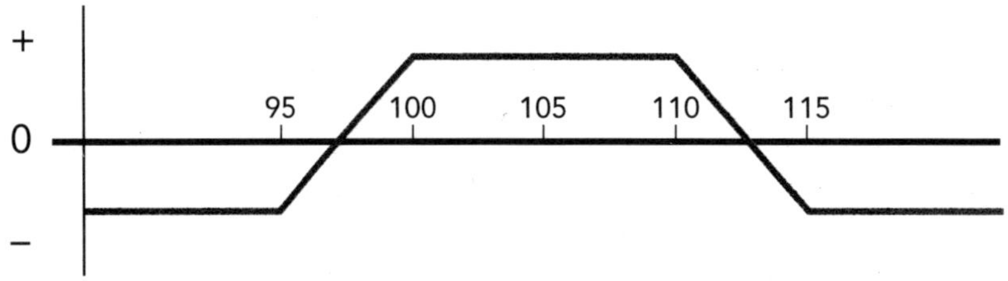

Composition: Long 1 95 call
Short 1 100 call
Short 1 110 call
Long 1 115 call
Same expiry, same underlying
Max Profit: (100 – 95) – 2.10 = 2.90
Max Loss: 2.10
Breakevens:
Downside: 95 + 2.10 = 97.10
Upside: 115 – 2.10 = 112.90

Figure 7.16 Diagram of the Long XYZ April 95/100/110/115 Call Pterodactyl *Source: Corona Derivatives, LLC*

"What If?" Scenarios (Potential Outcomes at Expiration)

Stock Price of 95.00	Long 1 XYZ April 95 call value	=	$0.00
	Short 1 XYZ April 100 call value	=	$0.00
	Short 1 XYZ April 110 call value	=	$0.00
	Long 1 XYZ April 115 call value	=	$0.00
	Net value of spread	=	$0.00
	Cost of spread	=	$2.10
	Net profit/loss	**=**	**–$2.10**
Stock Price of 97.10	Long 1 XYZ April 95 call value	=	$2.10
	Short 1 XYZ April 100 call value	=	$0.00
	Short 1 XYZ April 110 call value	=	$0.00
	Long 1 XYZ April 115 call value	=	$0.00
	Net value of spread	=	$2.10
	Cost of spread	=	$2.10
	Net profit/loss	**=**	**$0.00**

Stock Price of 100.00	Long 1 XYZ April 95 call value	=	$5.00
	Short 1 XYZ April 100 call value	=	$0.00
	Short 1 XYZ April 110 call value	=	$0.00
	Long 1 XYZ April 115 call value	=	$0.00
	Net value of spread	=	$5.00
	Cost of spread	=	$2.10
	Net profit/loss	**=**	**$2.90**
Stock Price of 105.00	Long 1 XYZ April 95 call value	=	$10.00
	Short 1 XYZ April 100 call value	=	–$5.00
	Short 1 XYZ April 110 call value	=	$0.00
	Long 1 XYZ April 115 call value	=	$0.00
	Net value of spread	=	$5.00
	Cost of spread	=	$2.10
	Net profit/loss	**=**	**$2.90**
Stock Price of 110.00	Long 1 XYZ April 95 call value	=	$15.00
	Short 1 XYZ April 100 call value	=	–$10.00
	Short 1 XYZ April 110 call value	=	$0.00
	Long 1 XYZ April 115 call value	=	$0.00
	Net value of spread	=	$5.00
	Cost of spread	=	$2.10
	Net profit/loss	**=**	**$2.90**
Stock Price of 112.90	Long 1 XYZ April 95 call value	=	$17.90
	Short 1 XYZ April 100 call value	=	–$12.90
	Short 1 XYZ April 110 call value	=	–$2.90
	Long 1 XYZ April 115 call value	=	$0.00
	Net value of spread	=	$2.10
	Cost of spread	=	$2.10
	Net profit/loss	**=**	**$0.00**
Stock Price of 115.00	Long 1 XYZ April 95 call value	=	$20.00
	Short 1 XYZ April 100 call value	=	–$15.00
	Short 1 XYZ April 110 call value	=	–$5.00
	Long 1 XYZ April 115 call value	=	$0.00
	Net value of spread	=	$0.00
	Cost of spread	=	$2.10
	Net profit/loss	**=**	**–$2.10**

As the gap between the debit spread portion of the position and the credit spread portion of the position increases, so does the area of potential maximum profitability. See **Figure 7.17**. The initial cost to purchase the position also increases, thus lowering the maximum return and increasing risk. Even though the probability of success is higher, the risk/reward ratio suffers to the point where the strategy may not make sense for some traders.

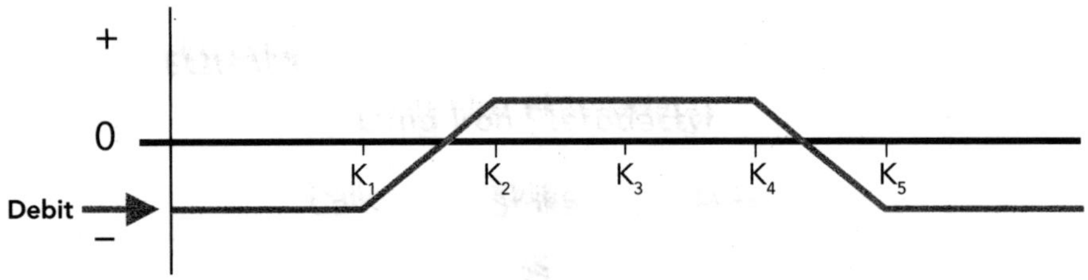

Composition:	Long 1 K_1 put Short 1 K_2 put Short 1 K_4 put Long 1 K_5 put Same expiry, same underlying
Max Profit:	$(K_2 - K_1)$ – debit
Max Loss:	Debit
Breakevens:	K_1 + debit; K_5 – debit

Figure 7.17 Long Put Pterodactyl P&L Diagram
Source: Corona Derivatives, LLC

Example

Buy the XYZ April 95/100/110/115 Put Pterodactyl:

- Buy 1 XYZ April 95 put at \$0.50
- Sell 1 XYZ April 100 put at \$2.00
- Sell 1 XYZ April 110 put at \$5.00
- Buy 1 XYZ April 115 put at \$9.50

This creates a long XYZ April 95/105/105/115 put pterodactyl at a debit of \$3.00 as shown in **Figure 7.18**.

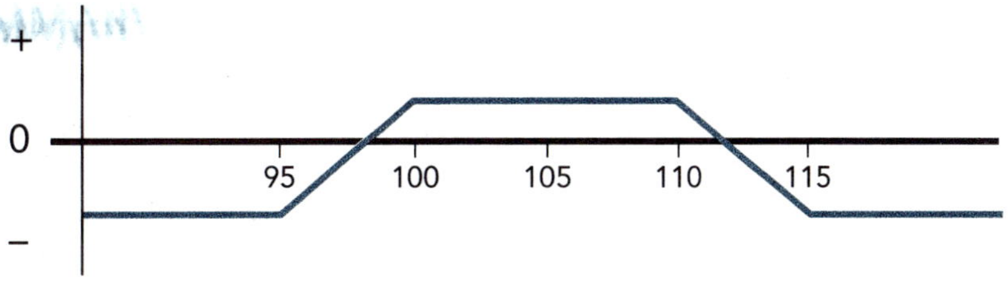

Composition:	Long 1 95 put Short 1 100 put Short 1 110 put Long 1 115 put Same expiry, same underlying
Max Profit:	(100 – 95) – 3.00 = 2.00
Max Loss:	3.00
Breakevens:	
Downside:	95 + 3.00 = 98.00
Upside:	115 – 3.00 = 112.00

Figure 7.18 Long XYZ April 95/105/105/115 Broken-Wing Call Condor Diagram *Source: Corona Derivatives, LLC*

"What If?" Scenarios (Potential Outcomes at Expiration)

Stock Price of 95.00	Long 1 XYZ April 95 put value	=	$0.00
	Short 1 XYZ April 100 put value	=	–$5.00
	Short 1 XYZ April 110 put value	=	–$15.00
	Long 1 XYZ April 115 put value	=	$20.00
	Net value of spread	=	$0.00
	Cost of spread	=	$3.00
	Net profit/loss	**=**	**–$3.00**
Stock Price of 98.00	Long 1 XYZ April 95 put value	=	$0.00
	Short 1 XYZ April 100 put value	=	–$2.00
	Short 1 XYZ April 110 put value	=	–$12.00
	Long 1 XYZ April 115 put value	=	$17.00
	Net value of spread	=	$3.00
	Cost of spread	=	$3.00
	Net profit/loss	**=**	**$0.00**

Stock Price of 100.00	Long 1 XYZ April 95 put value	=	$0.00
	Short 1 XYZ April 100 put value	=	$0.00
	Short 1 XYZ April 110 put value	=	–$10.00
	Long 1 XYZ April 115 put value	=	$15.00
	Net value of spread	=	$5.00
	Cost of spread	=	$3.00
	Net profit/loss	**=**	**$2.00**
Stock Price of 105.00	Long 1 XYZ April 95 put value	=	$0.00
	Short 1 XYZ April 105 put value	=	$0.00
	Short 1 XYZ April 110 put value	=	–$5.00
	Long 1 XYZ April 115 put value	=	$10.00
	Net value of spread	=	$5.00
	Cost of spread	=	$3.00
	Net profit/loss	**=**	**$2.00**
Stock Price of 112.00	Long 1 XYZ April 95 put value	=	$0.00
	Short 1 XYZ April 105 put value	=	$0.00
	Short 1 XYZ April 110 put value	=	$0.00
	Long 1 XYZ April 115 put value	=	$3.00
	Net value of spread	=	$3.00
	Cost of spread	=	$3.00
	Net profit/loss	**=**	**$0.00**
Stock Price of 115.00	Long 1 XYZ April 95 put value	=	$0.00
	Short 1 XYZ April 105 put value	=	$0.00
	Short 1 XYZ April 110 put value	=	$0.00
	Long 1 XYZ April 115 put value	=	$0.00
	Net value of spread	=	$0.00
	Cost of spread	=	$3.00
	Net profit/loss	**=**	**–$3.00**

As may be seen from the previous what-if scenarios and payout diagrams, the pterodactyl has a very wide area of maximum profit—10 points in the last two examples—but in order to get that high-probability profit, you have to pay for it and, in many cases, risk more than the potential maximum profit.

IRON PTERODACTYL

Chapter 6 discusses "iron" structures such as the iron butterfly and the iron condor. It shows that iron butterflies and condors are essentially synthetically equivalent to call and put butterflies and condors, with identical risk, reward, and break-even levels and amounts. The difference between the two types of winged structures is that long iron structures are constructed entirely of credit spreads, generating an initial credit when entering the position, whereas the long call or long put butterfly or condor is constructed of one debit spread and one credit spread, generating an initial debit when entering the position.

To the neophyte option trader, the choice of putting on a position for a credit versus a debit seems to be a no-brainer; a credit would always seem to be preferable. However, as seen in Chapter 6, this edge is really an illusion. Much of the popularity of these types of structures is built around the "always get a credit" concept, which can be misleading.

Currently, iron condors and iron pterodactyls are enjoying a lot of discussion on various websites and message boards. However, any winged structure can be "turned to iron" by substituting a synthetically equivalent credit spread for the debit spread portion of the position. **Figure 7.19** and **Figure 7.20** illustrate the link between a long call and long put pterodactyl and the "iron" pterodactyl.

Long Call Pterodactyl and Short Box Spread

Calls		Strike	Puts
+1	−1	95	+1
−1	+1	100	−1
		105	
−1		110	
+1		115	

EQUALS:

Long Iron Pterodactyl

Calls	Strike	Puts
	95	+1
	100	−1
	105	
−1	110	
+1	115	

Figure 7.19 Long Iron Pterodactyl Decomposition Diagram A
Source: Corona Derivatives, LLC

Long Put Pterodactyl and Short Box Spread

Calls	Strike	Puts	
	95		**+1**
	100		**–1**
	105		
–1	**110**	+1	**–1**
+1	**115**	–1	**+1**

EQUALS:

Long Iron Pterodactyl

Calls	Strike	Puts
	95	+1
	100	–1
	105	
–1	**110**	
+1	**115**	

Figure 7.20 Long Iron Pterodactyl Decomposition Diagram B
Source: Corona Derivatives, LLC

Once again, it is the short box spread that explains the difference between the debit and credit of the two synthetically equivalent positions. There are many reasons why a long iron winged structure might be preferable to a traditional long call or put winged structure. Some of these points are discussed in Chapter 8. However, it is very important to remember that at the point of execution, the initial debit or credit must be normalized by the value of the box structure in order to compare pricing across call, put, or iron structures.

SUMMARY

Popular mutant structures such as long "broken wing" call and put butterflies and condors, long pterodactyls, and long iron pterodactyls are simply variations of long call, put, or iron butterflies and condors. They usually are used for very specific market views.

Long Broken-Wing Butterflies or Condors

Long "broken-wing" butterflies and condors are simply long butterflies and condors with an extra credit spread added to the position in order to lower the cost of the structure. This creates an asymmetrical payout that increases the risk of the position in the direction of the credit spread, and reduces the risk of the position in the direction away from the credit spread. This type of spread usually is executed because the end user has a very specific market view that fits the asymmetrical risk/reward of this type of structure.

Long Pterodactyls and Long Iron Pterodactyls

A long condor can be viewed as two overlapping long butterflies. The long pterodactyl can be viewed as several overlapping butterflies. This causes the structure to have a large gap between the bull vertical spread and bear vertical spread portions of the position. The purpose of having a winged structure covering such a large area is to have a large maximum range of profitability; however, it also increases the risk of the position because each successive long butterfly added to the position increases the cost and thus the risk of the structure. The long iron pterodactyl is another synthetically equivalent "iron" structure in which the bull spread at the lower two strikes is a bull put spread, and the structure is composed entirely of out-of-the-money options. Once again, as is the case with long iron butterflies or long iron condors, the pricing of the long "iron" pterodactyl differs from the long call or long put pterodactyl by the pricing of the embedded box spread that causes this permutation.

CHAPTER 7 EXERCISE

1. The long broken-wing call butterfly has the embedded credit spread above or below the body?
2. The long broken wing call butterfly can be executed for a debit or credit. True or false?

For exercise questions 3, 4, and 5, refer to the position below.

May 100/105/115 broken-wing call butterfly
Buy 1 May 100 call @ $6.00
Sell 2 May 105 calls @ $4.00
Buy 1 May 115 call @ $0.40

3. Would the buyer receive a debit or credit when initiating the spread? How much?
4. Calculate the profit/loss at expiration, if the option's underlying security is trading at 95.
5. Calculate the profit/loss at expiration, if the option's underlying security is trading at 110.
6. At expiration, the broken-wing butterfly achieves the potential maximum profitability at the short strike. True or false?
7. The long broken-wing call butterfly takes its maximum loss at, above, or below the upper strike?
8. The long broken-wing call butterfly is usually placed at-the-money. True or false?
9. The long call condor is a combination of two vertical spreads. It can also be viewed as a bull spread adjacent to a bear spread. True or false?
10. The break-even points of the long broken-wing call butterfly at expiration are K_2 + debit, and K_3 −/+ debit (credit)? True or false?

CHAPTER 7 QUIZ

1. A long iron butterfly (condor) is constructed with debit or credit spreads?

2. What strategy is this?

   Long 1 K_1 call
   Short 2 K_2 calls
   Long 1 K_4 call

3. What strategy is this?

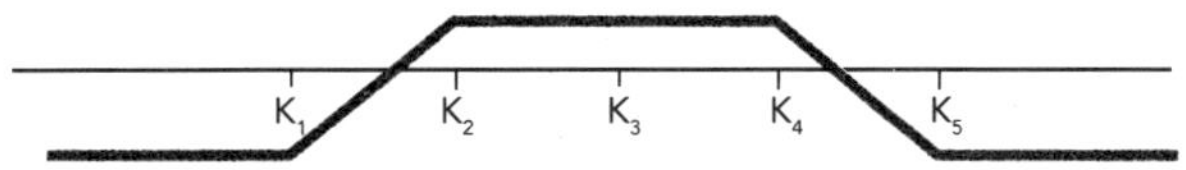

4. What strategy is this?

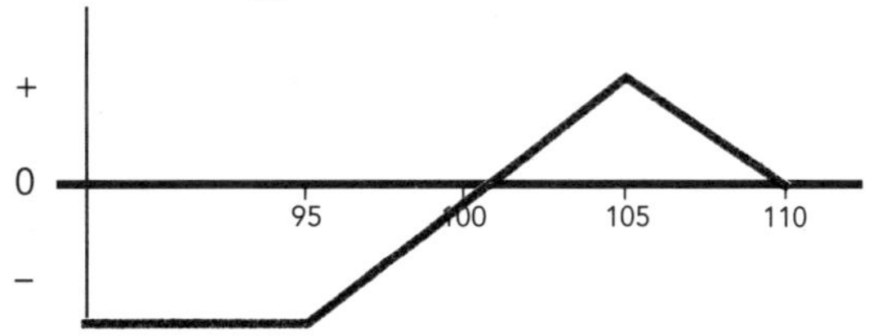

5. What are the breakevens for the long broken-wing put butterfly?

6. What is the maximum loss for the long call pterodactyl?

7. How do you calculate the potential maximum profit for the long call pterodactyl?

8. How do you calculate the maximum downside loss for the long broken-wing put butterfly?

9. How do you calculate the maximum upside loss for the long broken-wing call butterfly?

10. What are the breakevens for the long put pterodactyl?

Chapter 7 Exercise Answer Key

1. Above
2. True
3. Credit of $1.60 (–$6.00 + $8.00 – $.040)
4. All contracts expire worthless; therefore, keep the total credit of $1.60.
5. Credit of $1.60:

Long 1 100 call	=	$10.00
Short 2 105 calls	=	–$10.00
Long 1 115 call	=	$0.00
Net value of spread	=	$0.00
Cost of spread	=	$1.60 credit

6. True
7. Above
8. False. The broken-wing call butterfly usually has a directional bias. A long broken-wing call butterfly usually has a bullish bias and is placed above the underlying's price, so that the underlying has to move up through the area of potential maximum profitability *first*, before testing the area of potential maximum loss.
9. True
10. False: K_1 + debit (if any); K_3 –/+ (debit) credit

Chapter 7 Quiz Answer Key

1. Credit
2. Long broken-wing call butterfly
3. Long call or put pterodactyl
4. Long broken-wing put butterfly
5. Downside breakeven is K_2 (+)– (debit) credit; upside breakeven is K_4 – debit (if any)
6. Debit incurred to initiate the spread
7. $K_2 - K_1$ – debit
8. $(K_2 - K_1)$ –(+) credit (debit)
9. $(K_4 - K_3)$ –(+) credit (debit)
10. K_1 + debit; K_5 – debit

8 Strategy Application

CONCEPT REVIEW

Delta. The sensitivity (rate of change) of an option's theoretical value (assessed value) to a $1 (1-point) change in the price of the underlying instrument.

Gamma. The sensitivity (rate of change) of an option's delta with respect to a 1-point change in the underlying's price.

Theta. The sensitivity (rate of change) of theoretical option prices to changes in time. Theta measures the decay in the value of an option over one day in time.

Vega. The sensitivity (rate of change) of an option's theoretical value to a 1 percent change in implied volatility.

Vertical spread. The simultaneous purchase and sale of options with the same class and expiration, but with different strike prices. Depending on which strike is bought and which strike is sold, this type of spread may have either a bullish or bearish bias. For example: the XYZ July 100/105 call vertical spread. A bullish trader would buy the 100 call and sell the 105 call; a bearish trader would buy the 105 call and sell the 100 call.

Bear spread. A vertical spread with a bearish bias where one purchases a higher strike option and sells a lower strike option of the same class and expiration. A bear spread using calls (also known as a *short call spread*) will result in a credit, and a bear spread using puts (also known as a *long put spread*) will result in a debit.

Bull spread. A vertical spread with a bullish bias where one purchases a lower strike option and sells a higher strike option of the same class and expiration. A bull spread using calls (also known as a *long call spread*) will result in a debit, and a bull spread using puts (also known as a *short put spread*) will result in a credit.

Straddle. A strategy that involves the sale (or purchase) of an equal number of puts and calls with the same underlying instrument, strike price, and expiration date.

Strangle. A strategy that involves the purchase (or sale) of an equal number of puts and calls with the same underlying and expiration, but with different strikes. These strikes are out-of-the-money (unlike guts) and are usually, but not always, bracketing the current price of the underlying.

LONG BUTTERFLY AND CONDOR TRADING STRATEGIES

Scenarios suitable for the application of long butterfly and condor strategies can be broken into different categories. Chapter 1 notes that one of the many possible advantages of using options is the opportunity to build a customized strategy to fit a particular market view. The long butterfly and condor strategies are good examples of strategies that can be adapted to many different market scenarios, including the directionless market scenario. Regardless of the scenario or how it evolves, ultimately certain conditions need to be met for the long butterfly or condor positions to be successful:

- Movement toward the middle strike(s)
- Time decay
- Declining implied volatility

Movement Toward the Middle Strike(s)

The movement of the underlying's price toward the body (the short middle strikes) of this structure is the most important ingredient for the success of a long butterfly or condor position. For a long butterfly or condor to benefit from time decay, or from a decline in implied volatility, it has to be located so that the underlying's price is at or near the short middle strike(s), the body of the structure (i.e., in the *range of profitability*). If the underlying's price is away from the middle strikes, out near the wings or beyond, time decay and/or falling implied volatility will work *against* a long butterfly or condor.

Time Decay

The Greeks are introduced in earlier chapters, which also illustrate how a properly placed long butterfly or long condor position—one where the body of the position is at or near the current price of the underlying—will have positive time decay, quantified by theta. In other words, theoretically, the value of the long butterfly or condor should increase every day, provided the other market conditions remain unchanged. **Figure 8.1** and **Figure 8.2** demonstrate the change in price of a long butterfly and a long condor against the passage of time, given various prices of the underlying.

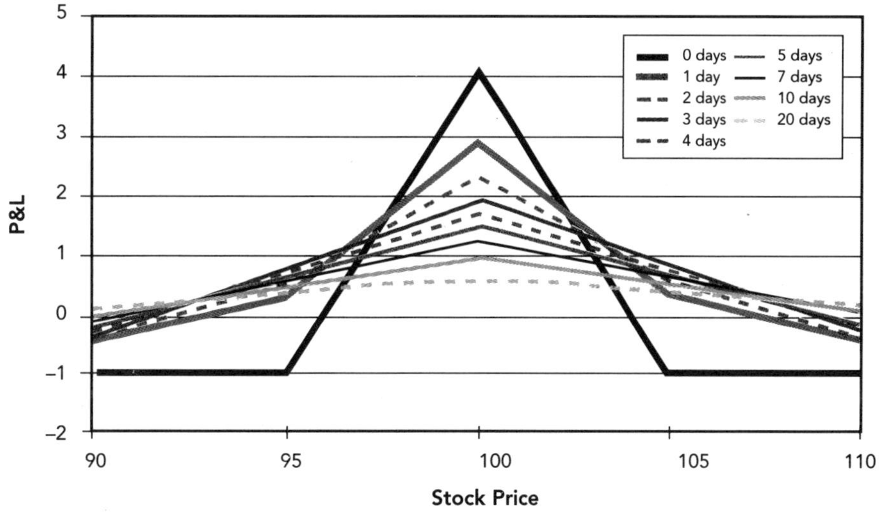

Figure 8.1 Long 95/100/105 Butterfly vs. Time
Source: Corona Derivatives, LLC

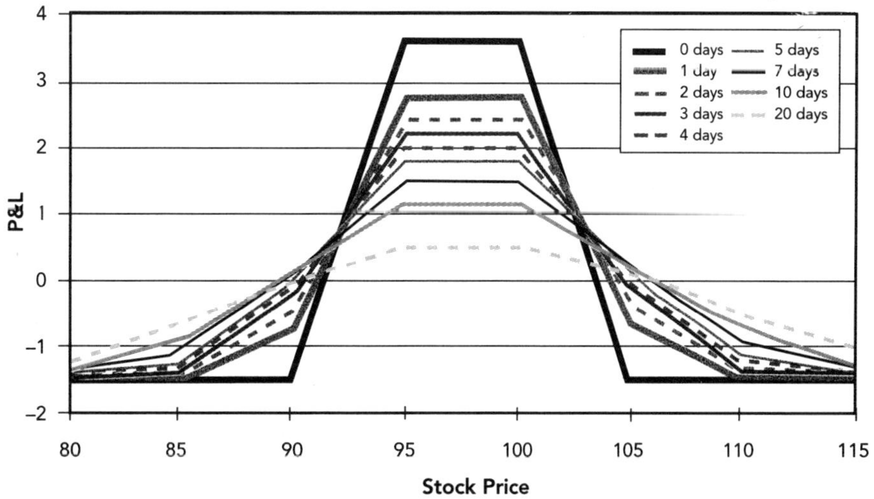

Figure 8.2 Long 90/95/100/105 Condor vs. Time
Source: Corona Derivatives, LLC

Declining Implied Volatility

Previous chapters examined the concept of declining implied volatility mimicking the passage of time and having the same effect on options and option structures. A properly placed long butterfly or long condor position (one where the body of the position is at or near the current price of the underlying) will have a negative exposure to changes in implied volatility, quantified by vega. In other words, theoretically, the value of the long butterfly or condor should increase as implied volatility falls, provided other market conditions remain unchanged. **Figure 8.3** and **Figure 8.4** illustrate the change in price of a long butterfly and long condor against falling implied volatility, given various prices of the underlying.

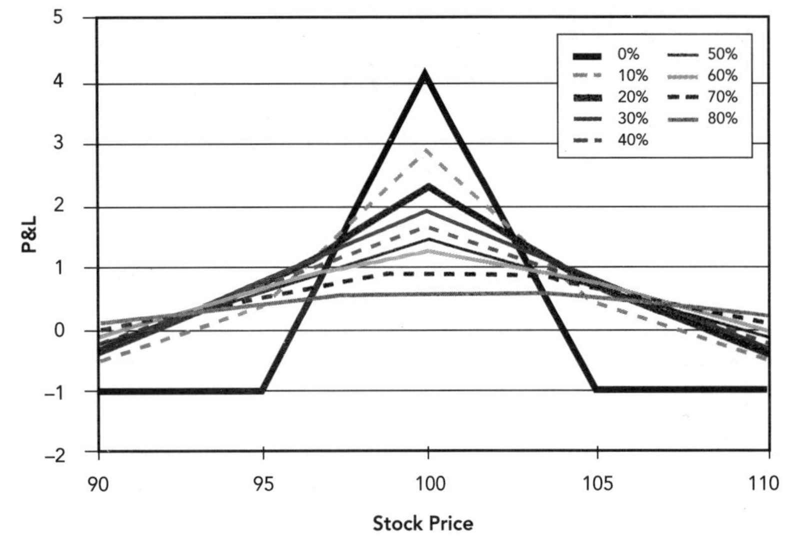

Figure 8.3 Long 95/100/105 Butterfly vs. Implied Volatility
Source: Corona Derivatives, LLC

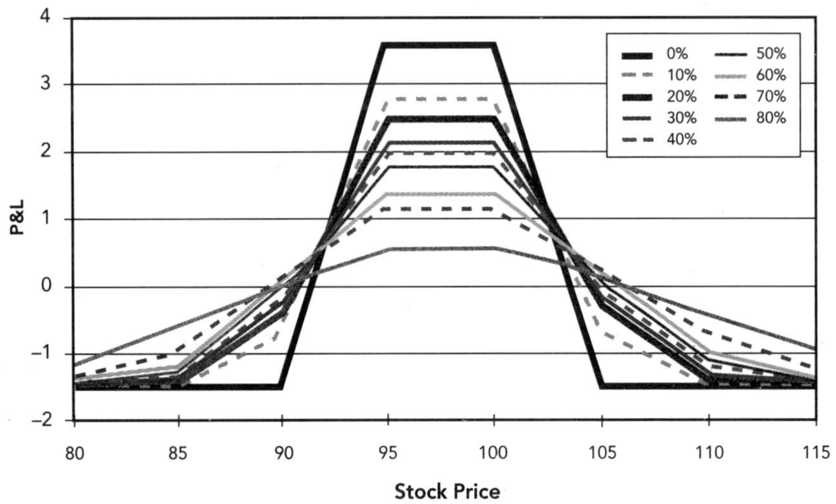

Figure 8.4 Long 90/95/100/105 Condor vs. Implied Volatility
Source: Corona Derivatives, LLC

COMMON TRADING SCENARIOS

There are many possible scenarios in which a long butterfly or condor strategy may be applied. Any market behavior that results in the underlying's price arriving at a certain price level at a certain time, or arriving at a certain price level with implied volatility declining, theoretically will lead to an increase in value of a properly placed long butterfly or condor structure. This section explores some of the more common scenarios to which a long butterfly or condor strategy might be applied.

Sideways Market (Time Transition)

In the sideways market scenario, the *location* requirement of the position has already been met. The underlying is already where the trader expects it to be at expiration. The trader is expecting the underlying to continue to move within its trading range, or possibly to gravitate to a particular strike within the range, through expiration. **Figure 8.5** shows an example of a sideways market. In this scenario the trader will be looking to profit from the effects of time decay, which will increase the value of a long butterfly or condor *if it is properly located*.

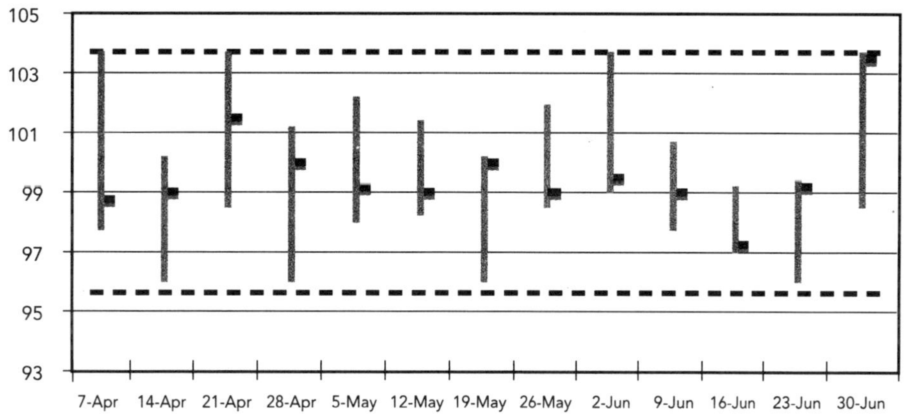

Figure 8.5 Sideways Market *Source: Corona Derivatives, LLC*

• Strategy Selection

With the underlying's price moving sideways within a trading range, the information needed for strategy selection is:

- Support and resistance levels
- Mean-reversion price (or area)
- Projected time in trading range

- **Strike Selection**

Support and resistance levels and mean-reversion price (or area) also are needed for strike selection. It is important to cover the trading range with the *range of profitability* of the long butterfly or condor. If the underlying's price is moving sideways through a narrow range and seems to revert to a particular price, *and* there is a strike price available at that particular price, it's an opportunity to construct a long butterfly position with the body (the short middle strike) at that price. It is also important to locate the wings (the long outer strikes) near the support and resistance levels to limit risk in case of a breakout from the trading range. In **Figure 8.6**, the underlying's price is moving sideways in a range between 97.50 (support) and 102.50 (resistance) with 100.00 seeming to be the mean reversion point. In this case a long 97.50/100/102.50 butterfly would make sense.

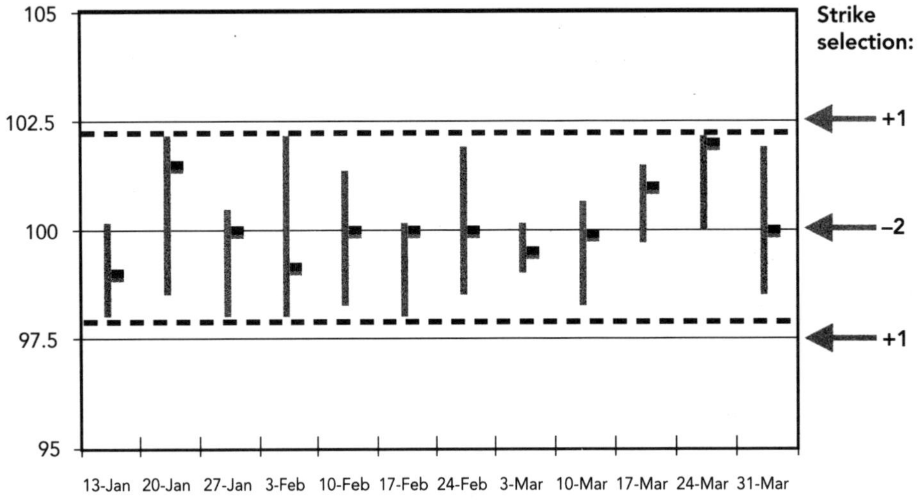

Figure 8.6 Narrow Range of Profitability *Source: Corona Derivatives, LLC*

If the underlying's price is moving through a wider trading range, and seems to mean-revert to an area or zone rather than a particular price, or if available strike prices do not match up well against important price levels, the strategy may be stretched into a long condor (or even a pterodactyl) to fit the range. In **Figure 8.7**, the underlying's price is moving sideways in a range between 195.00 (support) and 210.00 (resistance) with the 200.00 to 205.00 zone seeming to be the mean-reversion *area*. In this case a long butterfly does not have a large enough *range of profitability* to cover this area. A long 195/200/205/210 condor may be a better selection.

- **Expiry Selection**

A forecast of projected time in the trading range is necessary for selection of the expiration month. If the trader is estimating that the trading range will persist for thirty days, then he would need to use options that

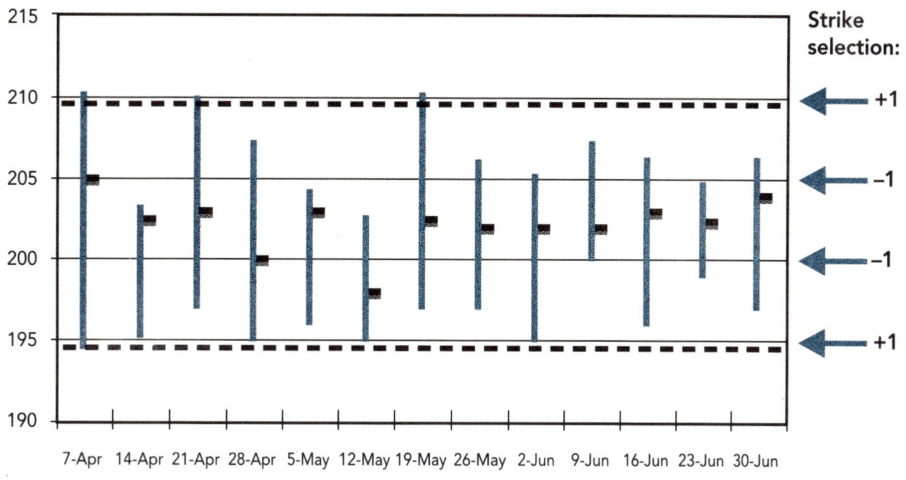

Figure 8.7 Wide Range of Profitability *Source: Corona Derivatives, LLC*

expire before that time. If he is forecasting a trading range that will persist for some time, though, which expiration should he choose? Long butterflies and condors made up of closer-dated options will bear fruit more quickly than their further-dated cousins (assuming the forecast of the trading range is correct). However, they also may be more risky and costly. If, for example, the forecast is for the trading range to persist for ninety days, it might be better to use a blend of the expirations occurring in that time period.

High Volatility to Low Volatility Transition

In the high volatility to low volatility transition scenario, the trader is anticipating a transition from a high-volatility environment to a low-volatility environment. This scenario usually (although not necessarily) involves a sharp move due to some type of news, followed by a price consolidation. This type of activity could have several explanations. It could be:

- **seasonal,** moving from an active time of year to a slower time of year, such as April earnings into the spring vacation season, July earnings into August vacation season, or October into the late November to December holiday season
- **post-earnings,** when the volatile periods associated with earnings announcements give way to slower post-earnings trade
- **post-event,** when consolidation periods follow volatile news shocks

In this scenario the trader will be looking to profit from the effects of declining implied volatility, which will increase the value of a long butterfly or condor *if it is properly located*. **Figure 8.8** is an example of a market transitioning from high volatility to low volatility. In this example, sharp price movement is followed by consolidation.

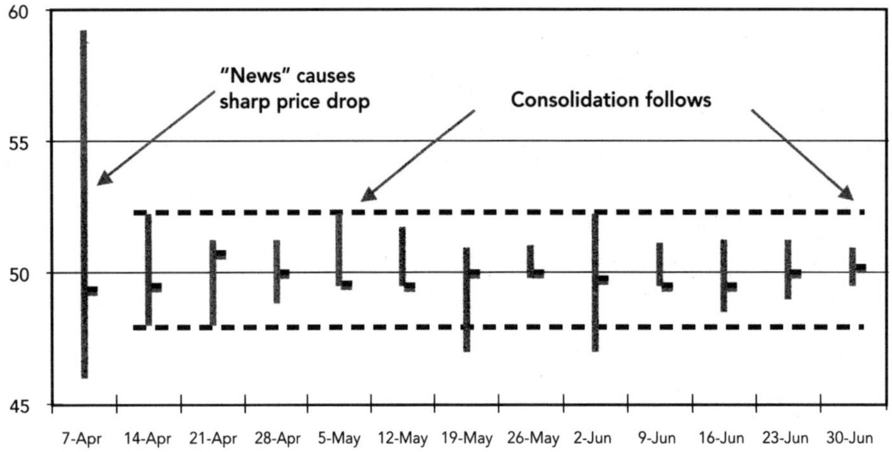

Figure 8.8 Declining Volatility Trading Range
Source: Corona Derivatives, LLC

- **Strategy Selection**

The difficult part of this type of trade is forecasting the price area in which the underlying will trade when the implied volatility begins declining. In order for a long butterfly or condor to benefit from declining volatility, the *range of profitability* must cover the trading range of the underlying. Traders may use tools such as historical support and resistance levels, Fibonacci retracement levels, Market Profile distributions, or any other statistical and technical techniques in an effort to identify the new trading range. In the end, however, the process is very subjective. Once the trader is comfortable with his forecast of the new trading range, strategy selection continues in the same manner as with the sideways market (time transition) scenario discussed above.

Price Transition I

In the price transition I scenario, the trader is anticipating movement in the price of the underlying from one area to another. This scenario usually occurs when the price of the underlying is in a trending mode, moving directionally, and then consolidating for a period of time before moving again. **Figure 8.9** illustrates this type of behavior.

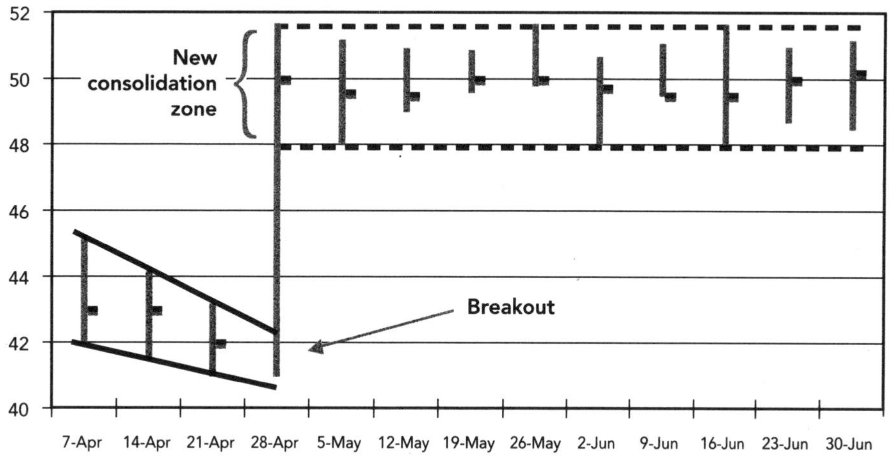

Figure 8.9 Price Transition Trading Range *Source: Corona Derivatives, LLC*

In this scenario the trader will be looking to profit from the impact of the *change in the underlying's price* on the value of the butterfly, followed by time decay and a possible decline in implied volatility, once the underlying settles into its new trading range. By purchasing the butterfly or condor before or during the move, while the underlying's price is still far away from the middle strike(s) of the position, the trader is able to buy it cheaply, and if the anticipated move to the body of the position takes place, the trader should theoretically realize a price increase. A bonus will be realized if the underlying's price then moves sideways for a time and/or implied volatility declines—both should add value to the long butterfly or condor position.

- **Strategy Selection**

Once again, the difficult part of this type of trade is forecasting the new price area in which the underlying will trade after the move. The technical tools mentioned in the high volatility to low volatility transition section often are used. Ultimately the decision rests with the trader, and once he is comfortable with his forecast of the new trading range, strategy selection continues in the same manner as with the previous sideways market and high volatility to low volatility transition scenarios.

Price Transition II

In the price transition II scenario, the trader again is taking advantage of movement in the underlying's price, but within a broad trading range. As the underlying's price approaches the support and resistance levels of the trading range, the trader will execute long butterfly (condor) positions, anticipating a reversion to the mean price or price area. **Figure 8.10** illustrates this type of behavior.

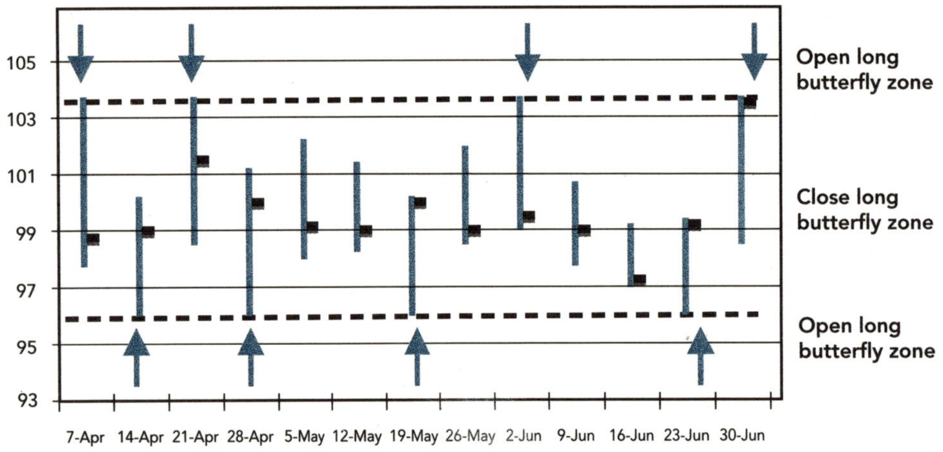

Figure 8.10 Price Rotation Trading Range *Source: Corona Derivatives, LLC*

As with the price transition I scenario, the trader is looking to profit from the impact of the *change in the underlying's price* on the value of the butterfly (condor), followed by time decay and a possible decline in implied volatility, once the underlying reverts back to its mean price or price zone within the trading range. By purchasing the butterfly or condor at the extremes of the trading range, while the underlying's price is still far away from the middle strike(s) of the position, the trader may be able to buy it more cheaply. If the anticipated reversion of the underlying's price to the body of the position structure takes place, the trader should theoretically realize a price increase. A bonus also may be realized if the underlying then moves sideways for a time and/or implied volatility declines—both should add value to the long butterfly or condor position. This scenario is a candidate for a long iron butterfly or condor "scalping" strategy, trading the underlying's price range by executing the position in stages (more on that strategy in the section that follows).

- **Strategy Selection**

The strategy selection process for the price transition II scenario is the same as for the sideways market (time transition) scenario.

IRON BUTTERFLY TRADE APPLICATION

As mentioned previously, the peculiar structure of the long iron butterfly (condor) makes it a potential trading vehicle. Some of its attributes:

- One bull spread, one bear spread.

- Both vertical spreads are out-of-the-money.

- Both vertical spreads have a low volatility bias.
- Long strangle, short straddle are embedded in the structure.

The fact that the long iron butterfly (condor) has so many basic options strategies embedded in it makes it a candidate for "build as you go" positioning. It can be assembled and disassembled in stages in order to capture an evolving market view. Bullish, bearish, or high- and low-volatility subcomponents can be added to or subtracted from the structure as one sees fit. Also, the fact that all of the options involved begin as out-of-the-money options means that they may have a tighter bid-ask spread and better liquidity than their in-the-money counterparts.

The following are examples of scenarios involving the gradual evolution of market views, and how the long iron butterfly (condor) framework may be utilized to exploit those views by adding or subtracting various subcomponent positions.

Bullish to Sideways to Bullish

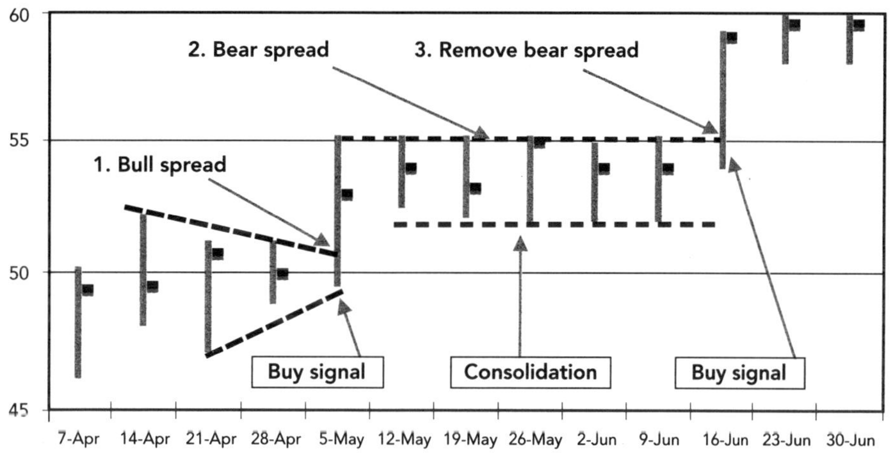

Figure 8.11 Bull Put Spread Evolution *Source: Corona Derivatives, LLC*

Stage 1. The trader receives a "buy" signal from his trading system and decides to put on a bull spread. Taking advantage of the liquidity and the narrow bid-ask spread of the out-of-the-money puts, the trader executes a bull put spread.

Call	Strike	Put
	50	**+1**
	55	**–1**

Stage 2. The trader's forecast is correct and the market rallies. However, the market has now come up against significant resistance, and the trader believes the market may consolidate and go sideways for a while. The trader adjusts the position by adding a bear call spread, converting the position to a long iron butterfly.

Call	Strike	Put
	50	**+1**
–1	**55**	**–1**
+1	**60**	

Stage 3. After a period of consolidation, once again the trader becomes bullish and closes the bear spread portion of the long iron butterfly, converting it back into a bull spread.

Call	Strike	Put
	50	**+1**
+1 –1	**55**	**–1**
–1 +1	**60**	

Bullish to Sideways to Bearish

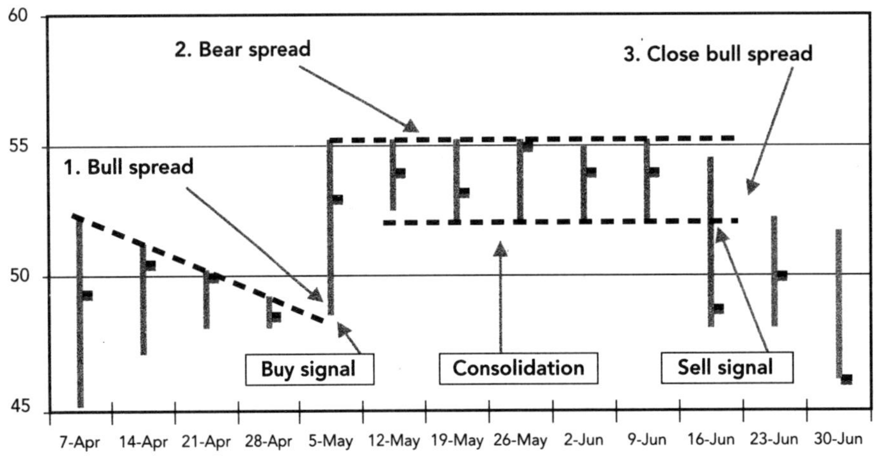

Figure 8.12 Bull Spread to Bear Spread Evolution
Source: Corona Derivatives, LLC

Stage 1. The trader receives a "buy" signal from his trading system and decides to put on a bull spread. Taking advantage of the liquidity and the narrow bid-ask spread of the out-of-the-money puts, the trader executes a bull put spread.

Call	Strike	Put
	50	+1
	55	–1

Stage 2. The trader's forecast is correct and the market rallies. However, the market has now come up against significant resistance, and the trader believes the market may consolidate and go sideways for a while. The trader adjusts the position by adding a bear call spread, converting the position to a long iron butterfly.

Call	Strike	Put
	50	+1
–1	55	–1
+1	60	

Stage 3. After a period of consolidation it appears a top is forming in the market. The trader becomes bearish and closes the bull spread portion of the long iron butterfly, converting it into a bear spread.

Call	Strike	Put
	50	–1 +1
–1	55	+1 –1
+1	60	

Bearish to Sideways to Bearish

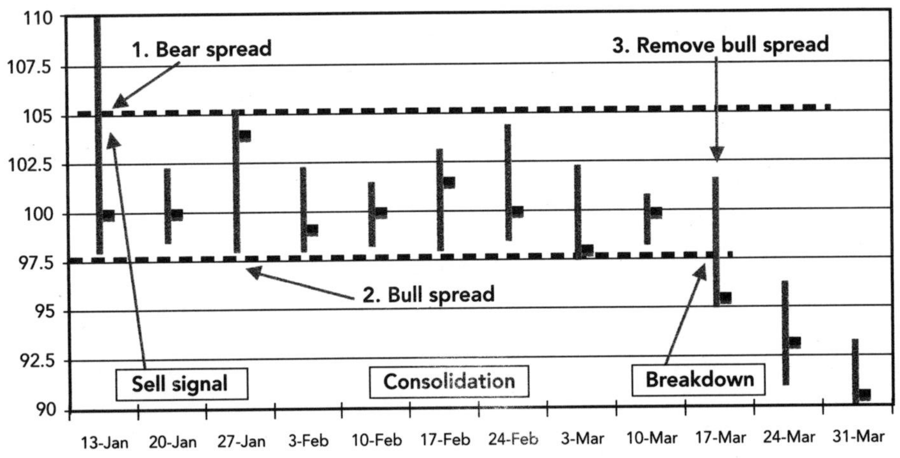

Figure 8.13 Bear Call Spread Evolution Source
Source: Corona Derivatives, LLC

Stage 1. A trader's research makes him bearish on a particular stock, and he decides to put on a bear spread. Taking advantage of the liquidity and narrow bid-ask spread of the out-of-the-money side, he executes a bear call spread.

Call	Strike	Put
–1	55	
+1	60	

Stage 2. The trader's forecast is correct and the stock drops to a strong support level. The trader believes the market may consolidate at these levels and begin to move sideways. The trader adds a bull put spread to the position, converting it to a long iron condor.

Call	Strike	Put
	45	+1
	50	–1
–1	55	
+1	60	

Stage 3. After a period of consolidation the trader believes the stock is going to start dropping again and closes the bull spread portion of the long iron condor, converting the position back into a bear spread.

Call	Strike	Put
	45	–1 +1
	50	+1 –1
–1	55	
+1	60	

Bullish to Long Volatility

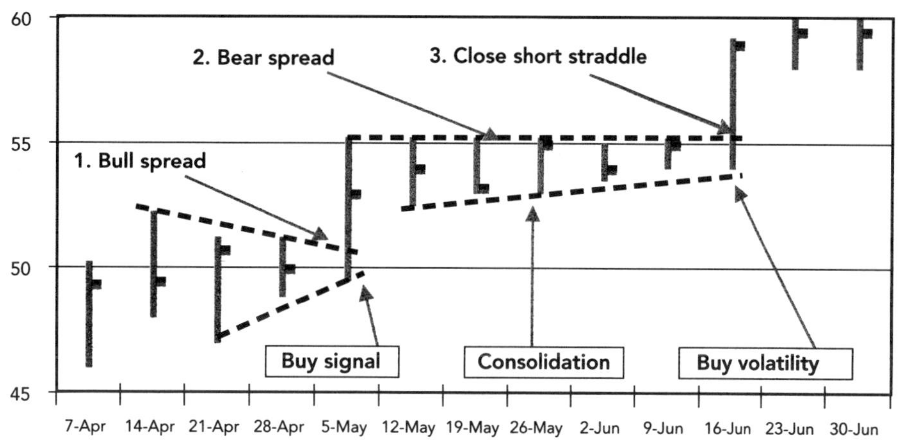

Figure 8.14 Bull Put Spread Evolution *Source: Corona Derivatives, LLC*

Stage 1. The trader receives a "buy" signal on the stock and executes a bull put spread.

Call	Strike	Put
	50	+1
	55	–1

Stage 2. The trader's forecast is correct and the market rallies. The trader now believes that a trading range might be developing and "caps" his position with a bear call spread, converting the position into a long iron butterfly.

Call	Strike	Put
	50	+1
–1	55	–1
+1	60	

Stage 3. Implied volatility declines sharply to the point where the trader believes the volatility is again a "buy." The trader liquidates the short straddle component of the long iron butterfly, converting the position into a long strangle.

Call	Strike	Put
	50	+1
+1 –1	55	+1 –1
+1	60	

Bearish to Short Volatility[1]

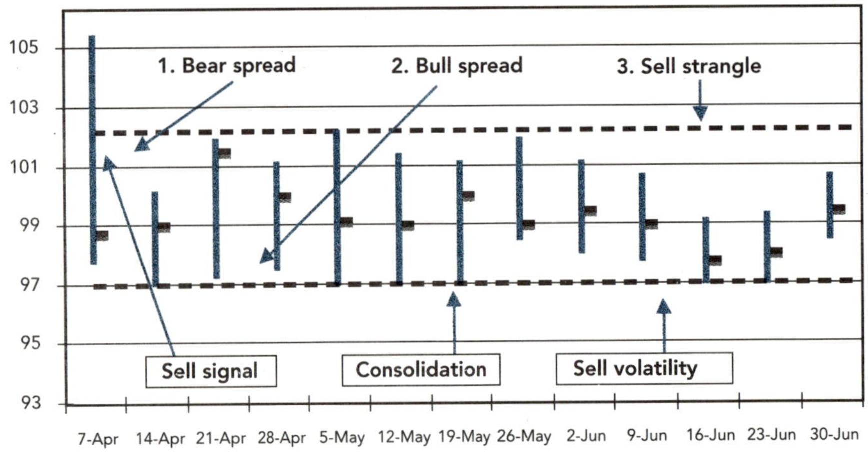

Figure 8.15 Bear Call Spread Evolution *Source: Corona Derivatives, LLC*

Stage 1. The trader receives a "sell" signal in the stock and executes a bear call spread.

1. Warning: This strategy evolves into a short straddle—an unlimited risk position not suitable for most investors!

Call	Strike	Put
–1	55	
+1	60	

Stage 2. The stock declines into a support zone, and the trader feels the stock may begin to move sideways in a consolidation phase. The trader adds a bull put spread to the position, converting it to a long iron butterfly.

Call	Strike	Put
	50	+1
–1	55	–1
+1	60	

Stage 3. Implied volatility rises to a level that the trader believes is a sale. He closes the long strangle portion of the iron butterfly, converting the position into a short straddle.

Call	Strike	Put
	50	–1 +1
–1	55	–1
–1 +1	60	

SUMMARY

The key to all of the butterfly (condor) strategies discussed in this chapter is capturing a *transition*, a particular change in market conditions that adds to the value of a long butterfly or condor position. By correctly anticipating a change in market conditions, whether it is the underlying's price, time until expiration, or a decline in implied volatility levels, the trader may be able to realize a profit from a properly placed long butterfly or condor position.

The examples of the long iron butterfly or condor structure being used as a trading vehicle in order to address evolving market views are just a few of many possible scenarios. The iron butterfly or condor is a fairly stable structure; it makes a good "base" or "resting" position while the trader waits for the market to show its hand.

CHAPTER 8 EXERCISE

1. Name the three conditions that need to be met for the long butterfly or condor position to be profitable:

    a. ______________________

    b. ______________________

    c. ______________________

2. In order for a long butterfly to benefit from time decay, it must be located so that the underlying's price is below the middle strike. True or false?

3. If the underlying's price is near the wings or out even further, will time decay work for or against a long butterfly or condor?

4. Will a properly placed butterfly or condor (underlying's price is at or near the middle strike or strikes) have a positive or negative exposure to vega?

5. In a sideways market, what information is needed for strategy selection?

    a. ______________________

    b. ______________________

    c. ______________________

6. If the underlying is trading in a range between 100 (support) and 110 (resistance) and 105 is the mean-reversion point, which butterfly would probably make the most sense?

    a. 95/100/105

    b. 100/105/110

    c. 105/110/115

7. If the range of profitability of a long butterfly does not fully cover the expected trading range of the underlying, one might consider employing a long condor instead. True or false?

8. Time decay is quantified by gamma. True or false?

9. Identify this strategy:

Call	Strike	Put
	50	+1
–1	55	–1
+1	60	

10. A long butterfly that has the middle strike located at or near the underlying's current price will have a negative exposure to changes in implied volatility. True or false?

CHAPTER 8 QUIZ

1. If a trader has the 30/35 bull put spread on and wishes to now convert it to a long iron butterfly, he would add the ______/_____ bear call spread.

2. Assume a trader has on the long 50/55/60 iron butterfly position. He hears some news on the stock and becomes very bearish. What could he do to his position to convert it to a bear spread?

3. Name at least one scenario in which there might be a transition from a high-volatility level to a low-volatility level in an underlying instrument.

4. If a trader purchased the 60/65/70 put butterfly after he went long the 55/60/65 put butterfly, what would be the resulting position (strategy)?

5. In order for a long butterfly or condor to benefit from declining volatility, the range of profitability must cover the trading range of the underlying's price. True or false?

6. As an underlying's price approaches the support and resistance levels of a trading range, a trader could execute a long butterfly or condor where the range of profitability is located in the area of the underlying's prior trading range with the anticipation of a reversion to the mean price. True or false?

7. A properly placed butterfly (short the middle strike at or near the current price of the underlying), will have a negative exposure to changes in __________ _____________.

8. A trader decides to sell the 40/45 bull put spread. After a market rally, new resistance levels occur and now the trader thinks the market may go sideways for some time and therefore wants to modify the strategy. He could sell the 45/50 bear call spread in order to convert the position into an iron butterfly. True or false?

9. Consider the scenario in question 8. If the trader becomes bullish again, how could he convert it back to a bull spread?

10. A trader has the 40/45/50 iron butterfly on. After a period of consolidation, the trader becomes bearish. What could be done to convert the strategy to a bearish position?

Chapter 8 Exercise Answer Key

1. a. movement of the underlying's price toward the middle strike;
   b. time decay;
   c. declining implied volatility
2. False. It needs to be located at or near the middle strike.
3. Against
4. Negative
5. a. support and resistance levels;
   b. mean-reversion price (area);
   c. projected time in trading range
6. b.
7. True
8. False. Theta quantifies time decay.
9. Long iron butterfly
10. True

Chapter 8 Quiz Answer Key

1. 35/40
2. Close out the 50/55 bull put spread
3. Seasonal, post-earnings, or post-event
4. Long the 55/60/65/70 put condor
5. True
6. True
7. Implied volatility
8. True
9. Close out the 45/50 bear call spread
10. Close out the 40/45 bull put spread

9

An Interview with Anthony J. Saliba

Tony Saliba is known as one of the pioneers of the options industry, as well as one of the first to actively trade the butterfly strategy. His insights on the markets and the evolution of the butterfly spread will be of interest to traders everywhere.

Q&A

It would be interesting and instructive to look back on how market making in general and specific strategies such as the butterfly in particular have evolved.

I began trading options in the late seventies when computers, pricing models, etc., were practically unknown. They were definitely unknown to me, a young upstart who had been a clerk for four months, one year out of college. There were people who traded who did not even know that there was a "model" that had a rough ability to keep the values of the options "in-line" relative to each other.

In fact, many of the stocks listed on the Chicago Board Options Exchange (CBOE) at that time did not have puts. This caused the relationships to be even more esoteric, because you could not anchor to anything "on the other side." I got lucky because most of the stocks I traded were issued puts early on.

In general, trading was the Wild West because of this general lack of understanding about options. There have been plenty of books written about the early days, so I would not want to be boring or repetitive, but suffice it to say, in 1978, there were about one thousand people involved in the trading of options, and probably less than 10 percent of them even cared to use a model.

This had ramifications in and of its own, because without any interest in trading things closer to being in-line, someone trading on fair values could wait a long time (maybe even only at expiration) for things to be priced properly. Thus, a trader may not get paid until long after the strategy was entered into.

Nonetheless, the trader I clerked for had an approach to trading that depended on a model to a great degree. That meant as a clerk, I got to use the computer.

It was 1978, less than a year after the Commodore Personal Electronic Translator (PET) 2001 came out as an answer to time-shared computing, and we were logging into The Metro Center mainframe with our Texas Instruments (TI) keyboard terminals to calculate theoretical values of the positions we had. We'd punch in our day's trades and the aggregate value was printed out on the heat-sensitive paper that scrolled out of the back of the all-purpose keyboard.

At the time, no one brought values into a crowd. Even more important, very few trusted the values. After all, who knew how to calculate an implied volatility, or interpret a dividend stream? "Vol surface" was a term that was not to be uttered for at least another decade.

But my exposure to the mainframe's ability to point to some form of "order" in this life was going to be helpful down the road.

A few months later, when I began to trade, I had no specific approach to the marketplace whatsoever. "Seat of the pants" they called it back then. "Sell 'em when you can, not when you have to," was a basic catchphrase (the same applied to buying). This connoted the ability to just "outfox" the other guy.

There were all sorts of "strategies" that guys employed, but most of them had a bit of guesswork in them and a lot of luck.

After having a number of rough months under my belt, I decided to look for an anchoring strategy. I was looking for something that could be in the range of market making (the ability to quote a lot or most of the strikes) and not be too complicated to remember while in the trading pit.

How did the majority of market makers make money in the early days? Was it simply from the capture of the bid-ask spread, directional bets, or strategies?

There were spreaders who had longer holding periods: spreaders who put on intermediate to long-term positions and held them all the way until expiration. These spreads ran the gamut from verticals, ratios, and calendars. There were spread scalpers who focused on one particular spread and were the master of that spread and traded in and out of that spread, based on what they perceived to be undervalued and overvalued vis-à-vis the stock price. There were all-out premium sellers who did nothing but sell out-of-the-money options. They sold puts when they thought the market was going up, and sold calls when they thought the market was going down, and adjusted their positions by selling even more options if the market went against them (sold even more if the market was going down, and more puts if the market was going up against their core position).

A lopsided spreader is a trader that oversold the out-of-the-money options and constructed the spread to yield a credit. For example, ratio spreaders would buy at-the-money options and then sell multiple out-of-the-money options against them.

Directional speculators would build an option position, and then if they were wrong about the market direction, they would trade the stock in the opposite direction.

Later came the theoretical traders who would bring their reams of "fair value" sheets out in the crowd. Many traders thought they were nuts.

How did market makers "price" their bids and offers at that time?

Most guys looked at relationships to the underlying that were crude, such as an absolute differential or a simple ratio. In other words, they would create their own delta based on price relations that they had observed over the previous days or weeks. For example, a trader may have observed that when the underlying was at 50, the 50 calls were trading at approximately $2.00. He would then make his market 1¾ to 2¼ when the underlying was at 50. And then make incremental changes to his market as the underlying moved away from 50.

How did market makers and other professionals manage the risk in their positions without the sophisticated tools (Greeks, etc.) we take for granted today?

There were sheets produced by the clearing firm called PLOT summaries that would graph the profit and loss over price and time that had had an equivalent stock position (ESP). They were produced overnight, however, and were not that good. For example, if volatility started to move up or down and completely changed the characteristics of your position, they would be useless, because they would not be updated until the following evening.

Traders would also manage risk in terms of "raw units." In other words, the trader would calculate the net calls and net puts of the position (including the synthetic calls and synthetic puts generated by any underlying position and create brackets based on strikes). They would then focus on those brackets that would show where they had risk.

Eventually I "broke down" my position into groups of spreads whose risk parameters I understood well.

What "vanilla strategies" were commonly used at that time?

One-by-two spreads. For example, buying one at-the-money call and selling two out-of-the-money calls. Or buying one at-the-money put and selling two out-of-the-money puts. Traders would try to put these on for even money or a credit and then let time decay work for them, increasing the value of the spread.

Vertical spreads. For example, bull spreads and bear spreads using calls and puts in which the trader had a directional bias and would build a position that had appetizing risk/reward ratio where they could risk one dollar to make three dollars, if they were correct. Typically, these took the form of long call spreads if the trader was bullish and long put spreads if the trader was bearish.

Calendar spreads. For example, long and short call calendar spreads or long and short put calendar spreads. When the spread became overvalued or undervalued with respect to its historical observed range over time, you would take the opposition position. For example, if the trader had observed for the last year that the relationship between a 30-day at-the-money call and a 120-day at-the-money call ranged between 2½ and 3½, then the trader would initiate long positions in the 2½ area and short positions in the 3½ area, wait for mean reversion, and take profits. This is very similar to how traders behave today except that we had no benchmark for fair value other than our own observations.

Diagonal spreads. These are simply combinations of vertical spread and calendar spreads with a directional bias. So the trader would incorporate a "cheap" calendar spread with a vertical spread in order to create a directional position at a good price.

What techniques were used to deal with a sideways market at that time?

A lot of people were straight out naked-premium sellers, so these were the markets in which they flourished. For many traders this was the only style of trading they knew.

When options were first listed, only calls were available to trade and we were in the depths of the Jimmy Carter–induced bear market. So there were only calls, and the market only went down. So the only options traders that made money were sellers of calls. "Sell the '80s, buy a Mercedes" was a common saying at that time. Volatility was very low from about 1977 to 1982 and the premium sellers flourished. Those habits carried over even after puts were listed. So the conventional wisdom at the time for many was that the only way to make money trading options was to sell them. This changed quickly with a few surprise takeovers (Kennecott Copper anyone?) and the bull market of 1982.

Others used ratio spreads such as the "One-One-and-a-Ton" (vertical spread with enough out-of-the-money options to bring in a credit). For example, you would buy *one* vertical spread and sell a *ton* of out-of-the-money options to generate a credit. If the market moved sideways you would collect the credit.

Obviously, all these strategies were extremely risky, which many traders found out the hard way.

When did you first come in contact with the butterfly strategy?

I started experimenting with various one-to-one spreads late in my first year of trading. After looking at the blocks of theoretical values and how they reacted when being shocked for price, volatility, and time, I quickly realized the symmetry of butterfly spreads and time butterfly spreads. I realized I had some inventory that I had accumulated that actually was butterflies, and it was extremely stable. I began to use the butterfly as a trading vehicle as well as a positioning vehicle because of the stability it exhibited.

Was the butterfly/condor strategy commonly used by market makers or other professionals at the time?

In the late seventies, early eighties there were a few traders who understood and used the strategy deliberately. There were other "inadvertent" butterfly traders who used the strategy but didn't really understand it. Even traders who understood what the strategy was seemed to feel that it was somehow beneath them.

I know the butterfly/condor is your favorite strategy. How deeply did you research the behavior of the butterfly before you started using it?

When I decided I needed to get a theoretical "backstop" to what I thought was a low-risk, high-reward trading vehicle, I went to my TI interface to the mainframe. At the time, all you could get were theoretical values for the individual options; there was no notion of spreads in the database (which was really just a big calculator using the Black-Scholes model). I would call up and print out (in reams of scrolled paper) the values for all the strikes of Teledyne, for a 20 percent move in either direction, for today, a month from now and expiration (Remember, back then we only had expirations every three months.) and for volatility moves of 5 percent, 10 percent, and 20 percent.

I would get this big block of paper and figure out what the butterfly was worth at all these levels. It took me the whole night to assemble it and study the results. (Eventually, I realized I did not have to do it every night; that the values held up for a few days if the stock did not make a violent move.) I was not concerned about the interest rate too much because it was already in the high teens and the impact was phenomenal, only if it were to come down. Reagan hadn't been elected yet, when I started, and it did not seem that the current administration was going to do anything but send rates higher.

Armed with this three-dimensional block of values, I got a feel for where the butterfly at each strike would "breathe," where advantages came in to be an owner of them, and where they could be shorted and replaced by something else.

I would basically memorize the value ranges of all the spreads (the butterflies and the straddles and strangles or verticals that made them up). I wrote a trading card every night with the starting values (based on last night's close) and that was how I started the day. As I branched out to calendars and other relationships, my card took on more values, all color-coded for the risk each "package" carried.

That was the form of research available to me, a bootstrap collection of values and rote memory. I guess the majority of the effort was just in producing the spread values.

When using a butterfly or a condor, how did you decide when to put it on?

Based on my research, I had an idea of what butterflies were generally worth under all conditions such as high volatility, low volatility, time until expiration, and moneyness (how far the structure was from the current underlying price). I had a good idea of what the butterfly was worth under all these conditions. In other words, when they became undervalued, I would accumulate long positions, and when they became overvalued, I would accumulate short positions, always looking to take profits somewhere near "fair value" when reversion would occur. Sometimes due to market forces, some butterflies could be overvalued while others were simultaneously undervalued. When this occurred, I would buy the undervalued butterflies and sell the overvalued butterflies and build a position. In this way, I was using the value of the butterfly structure to reveal which options were theoretically overpriced or underpriced without using theoretical values. My knowledge of the values of the butterflies served as a filter to help me locate mispriced options, which I could then incorporate into a larger butterfly position.

- Due to a forecast of slow market conditions

When it was obvious we were heading for a slow patch, such as holiday time or summer markets, I would deliberately set myself up to accumulate long butterfly positions that would take advantage of the upcoming low volatility that I was expecting. Through the normal market-making process, I would try to make my markets in such a way so as to allow me to accumulate long butterflies.

- Risk management overlay for existing positions

I would also use the position as a buffer for other long option positions that I was using. For example, if I was expecting a large move up, I might have a position that was net long a lot of calls, such as a call backspread. A call backspread has unlimited profit potential to the upside but also has negative time decay. If I was nursing a large call backspread position, I would usually overlay long butterflies to help mitigate the effects of time decay. If the market exploded to the upside as I had forecast, the long butterfly overlay would generate a loss, but a limited loss, while the call backspread would explode into unlimited profit potential to the upside. Whenever I had long premium positions reflecting my directional view of the market and I was worried about the timing, I would usually overlay some long butterfly positions to help soften the impact of time decay.

- As a stable trading vehicle

My research indicated that under general conditions, the butterfly was a fairly stable structure. Because it is made up of an equal number of long and short options and one bull spread and one bear spread, it usually does not have large price swings as volatility ebbs and flows as time passes. Obviously, if volatility falls far enough or as expiration approaches, the butterfly structure becomes more sensitive. Most of the time, however, it is fairly stable. This made it an excellent trading vehicle. As I operated in the pit as a market maker, whenever I captured an edge I would attempt to build it into a butterfly in order to preserve as much of the edge as possible until the time I could take profits. The butterfly position was a safe haven for me. I was almost always trading in and out of some sort of butterfly structure. If anything happened suddenly, I knew I would be safe because my position had limited risk.

When a butterfly position was profitable, how did you decide when to take it off?

- Degradation of risk/reward ratio

Sometimes the price of the spread itself tells you when to exit. In the case of the long butterfly spread, when I had "milked it" to the point there was very little upside left in the position, there was nothing to gain by holding on to it, therefore I would liquidate it. At that point, the position was all risk and no reward and was not worth having. In other words, I had nothing to gain and everything to lose. Conversely, when I had a short butterfly position and the value was low and the risk/reward ratio was out of balance in the other direction, meaning the position could not go much lower, I would lock in profits and liquidate those positions. These were kind of "no-brainer" scenarios.

- Transition to a more volatile market
- Transition to a directional (trending) market
- Other

When the behavior of the market would begin to change, whether it began to move in a trend or became more volatile, or began to do something I didn't expect, I would have to make adjustments in my strategies. I no longer had the luxury of holding positions in inventory for long periods of time. I would have to turn over the inventory quickly. In these times, I would still use the butterfly position as a trading vehicle, but would tend to mix and match long and short butterflies into the position to add further stability to the overall position. I would then move these butterflies in and out of inventory as they "breathed" with market movement (both directional and volatility). When volatility would swing up depressing the value of all butterflies, I would liquidate short butterfly positions and inventory long butterfly positions. When volatility would swing back down, expanding the value of all butterflies, I would liquidate all long butterfly positions, and inventory short butterfly positions. I was always keeping an eye on the risk/reward ratio of the individual butterfly spreads themselves. Using this technique, I was able to operate within the butterfly structure even in volatile and directional markets.

What is the longest stretch of sideways markets you can recall?

Depending on the scale, the entire decade from 1975 to 1985, in which the major averages gyrated in a relatively tight range. But there were periods in 1985 in which the market sat for one expiry after another for the first nine months. Butterflies got to be fatter as this occurrence became expected—then that is when the market took off.

Were you a heavy user of the long butterfly strategy at that time?

Unfortunately, they were too expensive, in my opinion at the time. I had left the floor already, "retiring" on my thirtieth birthday, and was trading from off the floor. Legging into butterflies was not possible, so I refrained from buying them, outright. The trade that I was setting up was a ratio spread—in effect, selling the butterfly without buying the way out of the money.

When volatility levels got very low, did you tend to liquidate long at-the-money butterfly positions and acquire out-of-the-money butterfly positions due to the relative inequity of their risk/reward ratios?

When volatility levels got very low, a short volatility strategy such as a long butterfly would get expensive. This would make it unappealing from a risk/reward standpoint. First of all, I would liquidate any long butterflies I had accumulated in my inventory, because you would have very little upside in these positions and a lot of downside. That being said, volatility does trend just like anything else; and if volatility happens to be low, the chances that it will remain low for the near term are pretty strong. Therefore, a short volatility position was still desirable. This was a difficult position to be in. To work around this, I would try to use my advantage of being a market maker to build long butterfly positions at a superior price by capturing the bid-ask spread in the component options. This would give me a bit of a cushion and help to limit the risk to some degree. Under these conditions, I would always have an itchy trigger finger on these positions because of the poor risk/reward ratio. I would also try to accumulate cheap out-of-the-money butterfly positions that would expand if the underlying did begin to move in their direction.

When volatility levels are high and long butterflies are cheap, how would you approach the market/long butterfly trades?

When volatility levels are high, at-the-money butterflies get cheap, and I would liquidate any short butterfly positions I would happen to have in inventory. Once again, I would structure my market-making activity to deliberately accumulate cheap long butterfly positions in my inventory. From a risk/reward standpoint, this made sense. I was initiating limited risk, short volatility positions at low cost at a time when volatility was high. I was always very comfortable with this type of strategy and it treated me well.

Under high volatility conditions, did you tend to inventory cheap long butterfly positions as good risk/reward "bets?"

One of the biggest advantages a market maker has is the ability to "create," through the market-making process, positions that have limited, or in some cases, no risk, and then to inventory these positions. Over time, these bets would pay huge dividends as the market made unexpected low-probability moves that turned into huge payoffs for those with the right positions. These positions are effectively mini lotto tickets that have nothing or very little to lose and everything to gain. Butterfly positions were no different, and when volatility skyrocketed, crushing butterflies, it was a great time to inventory them. They can't go below zero, and sometimes you could buy them for pretty close to that price.

Obviously, you were enormously successful as a trader. What portion of your profitability was attributable to your mastery of the nuances of the butterfly position?

The butterfly position ultimately became pivotal. I started with it gingerly and then built around it. It became the core of large positions, anchoring both from a profit potential and as a mechanism off of which to trade.

I would say that rarely did I let a butterfly go to the last moment of expiration. I usually used the profit that the butterfly had in it, to parlay into a spread needed to leverage the overall position. I did experiment, at times, with holding closer to expiry a butterfly that had matured to a level of profit. It became another exercise altogether. That task was simply managing a short straddle.

Whereas the butterfly moved as a spread throughout most of the cycle, on the day of expiration, you were eyeballing two short positions and the P&L would shift on a tick-by-tick basis with the underlying. Mastering the skills of the ultimate premium sellers, those that came in the last day and shorted the ATM straddle, then had to become part of my repertoire.

Still, I owned the butterfly through the early nineties. I know it is a brash statement, but I drilled down so deep into the different permutations, that people were still coming to me to learn how to trade them in 1993, a couple years after I left the floor for good. The pregnant butterfly, a strategy that a former partner of mine, Charles Cottle, documented in detail in his books was born (pardon the pun) in my shop.

I took my second software program, which I designed and built in 1986, and configured it to synthesize butterflies, based on the fragments of the position at various strikes. We had to name the fragments for the program, and thus were created a number of new types of butterflies that made their way into the vernacular.

Elongated butterflies, ratioed butterflies, turbo butterflies, Tennessee butterflies, all were creations that I labeled so that I could communicate with my traders and programmers. So mastery was taken to a different level.

Can you walk us through some of your best butterfly trades?

Believe it or not, the trade that stands out most in my recollection, was a series of butterflies I put on that never saw the light of day—and expired a couple hundred points deep in the money (worthless).

It was during one of those really long sideways stretches I mentioned that happened in 1984. Teledyne had been trading in a very tight range between $75 and $85 for months. This was when we still had expiration cycles that were only every three months.

It was early April, the stock was at $78 and the July at-the-money butterfly was cheap at the time—or so it seemed. I was loading up on them to the point where I was nearing the position limits. As an additional strategy in case the stock moved, I was buying the July 85 calls for under $1 per contract.

There must have been something in the winds, to keep a butterfly so cheap, because on the morning of April 18, just after opening rotation, the company announced a tender offer for the majority of the outstanding shares at a price of $200 per share. Needless to say, the butterflies were almost immediately near worthless, as the stock stopped trading, and then reopened at $180 per share.

The July 85 calls, though, were a different story altogether. The $100 opening bid per contract more than covered the cost in the butterflies. There was a lot that went on after that, as the stock marched to over $300 per share, as one of the greatest short squeezes in U.S. equity history commenced. But it all started with that position, overloaded with cheap butterflies—and that is what I remember most.

Even though the conditions were unbelievably volatile, didn't the butterfly position play a key role in the profits you made from the crash? How so?

Similar to the positions I built while I traded in Teledyne in the early '80s, when I moved into the Standard & Poor's 500 Index (SPX) pit in 1986, I gravitated to the same style of inventory.

Throughout the first eighteen months in the SPX pit, I organized my position with a series of near-the-money butterflies. The SPX was not nearly as volatile as Teledyne, but due to the high dollar price of the index, the premiums were nothing to ignore.

During August of 1987, the market was approaching all-time highs. The S&P 500 was trading over 300 and there were lots of out-of-the-money puts. This meant that these low-priced little puts were ripe for putting together inexpensive butterflies.

While the index lurched higher, firms kept coming in and selling puts, although customers were mostly interested in buying them. I constructed a large, lopsided butterfly, one-to-one in units (the same number long as short), but a wider margin between the first long put and the first short put (middle) than between the middle put and the furthest leg. The highest strike was the December 300 put, while the lowest strike was the December 230, pretty far away from where the index was trading.

By early October, I was once again bumping up against the position limits. The bulk of the position was the out-of-the-money butterfly.

The market broke, correcting a bit in the first week of October, but the butterfly did not budge in price. When October 19 brought us the meltdown, the index went right through all my strikes, closing just pennies above 200. The out-of-the-money put that I was long, went from 1⁄16 ($0.0625) to $32.00 in one day. The butterfly was now on the other side of the spectrum being in the money.

The crash brought chaos to the firms' pricing models, with volatilities soaring over 100 in the indexes. The pricing sheets and machines in the crowd were useless. No one knew what volatility to use. It was nearly impossible to price an option in a vacuum.

On Tuesday, October 20, when the market opened significantly higher (up almost 15 percent), none of the machines had prices to open the option. The futures were open and trading wildly, but the parameters had been blown out too much for those using the model to make a price.

Now the index was on the doorstep of my butterfly's first strike, the 230s. Having a full inventory of butterflies, and having studied their values religiously, I single-handedly opened all the series, using relative pricing, based on butterfly relationships. With all those butterflies that I had, and the extra-wide markets that the exchange allowed us to make while the panic was still in the futures market, enabled me to make all those markets with confidence.

In doing so, I was able to move in and out of my butterflies with ease and at the prices that I wanted. Each of the butterflies became rich, profitable, and liquid, all while the other market makers were bewildered and scattered. It was the "perfect storm."

The crash seemed to be a turning point in the markets, with the lower-capitalized local traders or independent market makers gradually fading from the scene and being replaced with large, well-capitalized, and well-trained professional trading groups. These groups had large numbers of traders, used a lot of computing power, and used sophisticated pricing models and risk management techniques. How did you compete with these groups?

The fact that these groups tended to manage risk in large buckets left the door open for traders like me who had mastered the intricacies of specific strategies such as the long butterfly.

Even though these types of groups were successful on a large scale, their focus on the forest rather than the trees allowed a lot of profits to slip through the cracks, and into the pockets of traders such as myself. These organizations were very model dependent, and when the market behaved in ways that did not fit the model, they would sometimes have difficulty operating. It was times like these that a spread trader could outperform these types of traders. These organizations were not so nimble, and at that time, it took a long time for them to adapt to changes in the market.

The theoretical value sheets that were the bread and butter of these types of organizations took a lot of time to generate. When the market moved quickly, because they were relying on theoretical values that were already obsolete, individual traders such as me could outmaneuver them. We kept our "theoretical values" in our heads due to our knowledge of spread relationships. While they were waiting for new sheets, we continued capturing edges.

Eventually, as technology marched on and modeling, risk management techniques, and communications became more sophisticated, many more groups began to move into the option markets. This further tightened the bid-ask spreads and traders were forced to take on more risk in order to make decent returns. Taking more risk demanded more capital, and this forced many of the remaining independent market makers to band together into groups or to trade from "upstairs." The heyday of the independent market maker was over.

For many years, large trading groups had great advantages over the individual investor. They had access, information, and a very low cost basis that the individual investor could not hope to compete with. In recent years, technology and competition have erased this advantage to a large degree. Computers are faster, commissions are lower, and due to the Internet, the individual has almost equal access to market-moving information. In short, the playing field has almost been leveled for options traders. This has made more sophisticated option strategies available to the individual trader than ever. Is this the golden age of options trading for the individual options trader?

Yes and no. Yes, for all the reasons mentioned. It is a great time for an individual options trader, commissions have never been lower and technology has never been better. The advent of portfolio-based margining has given the individual options trader leverage almost equal to that of professionals. No, because no matter how good it is right now, it will continue to get better. Exchange and broker competition will continue to whittle away at costs, while technological innovation will give individual options traders greater access to more sophisticated strategies.

With the existence of electronic complex order books on the CBOE and the International Securities Exchange (ISE), is this the golden age of the spread trader?

Yes, this is the beginning of that golden age. I feel that options traders are just getting started. There will soon come a time when they are trading in and out of spreads and other complex structures as easily as they trade in and out of calls and puts today. Technological innovation will remove friction, increase access, and reduce bid-ask spreads in these markets, making it easier for the individual to get in and out quickly.

What steps should the traditional "buy calls if I'm bullish, buy puts if I'm bearish" individual options trader take to get in the spread game?

Get educated. Once it was difficult to find any organized options courses. That was my motivation for starting the International Trading Institute back in 1989. Nowadays, there are plenty of avenues available to the individual who wants education. There are classroom and online courses available, a plethora of books, CDs, videos, and other learning materials available. The exchanges and most brokers have excellent materials also. There is no excuse for not getting educated.

The long butterfly or condor position, properly located, gives the individual the ability to sell volatility at limited risk. Why don't more people use it?

In the past, it was very difficult for the individual to effectively trade such structures. There were four commissions to open the position (and maybe four ticket charges), four commissions to close the position (and maybe four more ticket charges), and you had to pay the bid-ask spread, which was usually a mile wide. This meant that as an individual options trader you would have to be a trading genius to make any money. You might have been able to make a little money if you were right, but God help you if you were wrong. Individual options traders were effectively locked out of these strategies.

Now commissions are much lower, ticket charges are disappearing, bid-ask spreads are tightening, and complex order books are removing entry and exit friction. These spreads are now in reach of the individual options investor, I think many of them just have not realized it yet. It will come.

Where can the individual investor find information on butterfly prices?

The best way to find information is to observe them in the marketplace. Get quotes and pay attention. Watch them online. Many broker websites now have "RFQ" (Request for Quote) functionality. Ask for quotes and study the indications in real time. Unfortunately, settlement prices can be misleading and should not be relied upon as an indicator of where structures such as butterflies or condors are actually trading.

Does one need to have a strong understanding of the Greeks to be a profitable spread trader?

It is not necessary to have a strong understanding of the Greeks, but the individual options trader should understand why and how these spreads move, as well as their risk, reward, and break-even levels. It is important to keep things simple; overanalyzing the Greeks of a limited risk/limited return structure such as a long butterfly can sometimes be counterproductive.

What last piece of advice do you have for traders in sideways markets?

It is important in all trading to be patient and take what the market gives you. Trying to "force" trades that are inappropriate for the situation, or because one is "bored" or "needs to make money" is a sure path to a losing trade. This is especially true in the case of sideways markets because they are, by definition, boring.

Wait for the market to define the boundaries of a congestion zone with support and resistance levels and project a time horizon that you are comfortable with. Identify the price or area where mean reversion seems to take place within the congestion zone and structure the strategy appropriately. After the trade is made, it must be managed; this is where patience and discipline really come to the forefront.

Because it is generally the passage of time that causes the properly located winged structure to appreciate in price, the investor must be willing to sit patiently with this type of position to allow this to occur. Jittery types will not do well with this.

It is just as important to monitor the market conditions and to act when they change. If the support and resistance levels are significantly penetrated, chances are that the underlying is going to move to a new location, which would hurt the value of a long butterfly or condor position. If this occurs, the assumption that the market was in a sideways condition is invalidated, and the position should be liquidated.

Risk/reward ratios should also be monitored closely. It is always best to put on positions with a low risk/reward ratio, meaning you are risking a little to make a lot. Also, if an existing position gets to be fully valued (very little upside potential remaining), it should be liquidated.

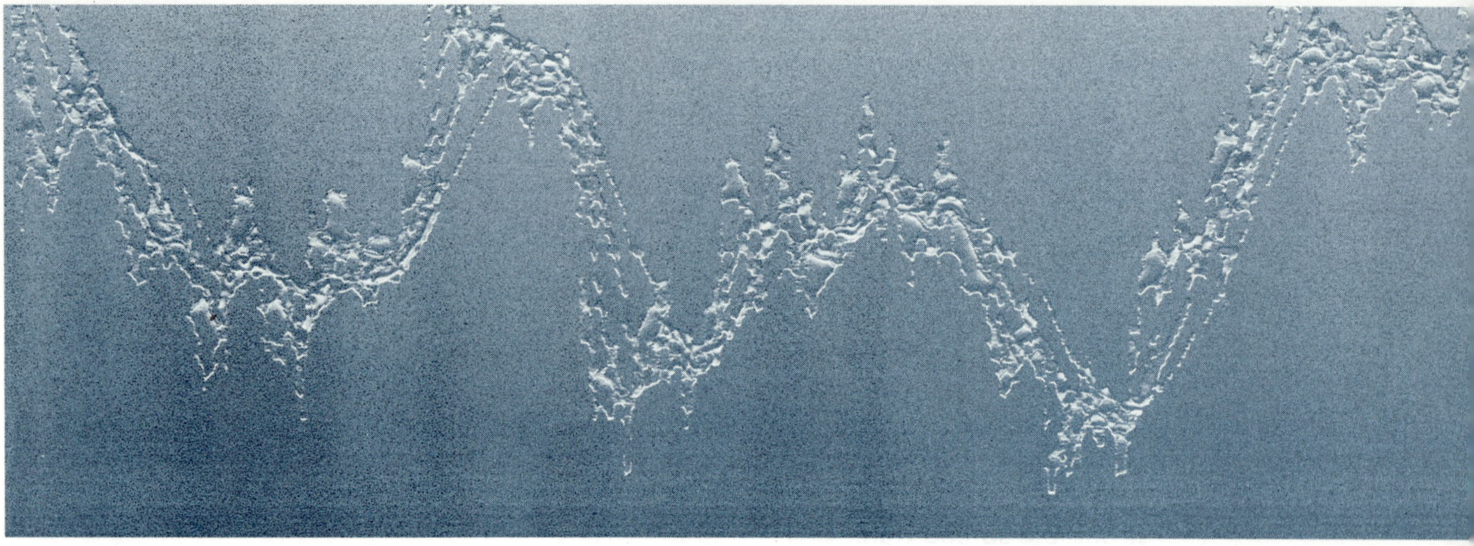

Appendix A

FINAL EXAM

1. Support is a price level below the current market price where buyers become more willing to buy and sellers are reluctant to sell. True or false?

2. Over time an option will eventually lose all of its extrinsic value. True or false?

3. Do short options have positive or negative theta?

4. Do in-the-money, at-the-money, or out-of-the-money options have the highest vega?

5. The amount of extrinsic value in an option depends on what five factors?

Given the butterfly position below, answer questions 6 to 10:

Long 1 XYZ 90 put @ $1.45
Short 2 XYZ 95 puts @ $2.80
Long 1 XYZ 100 put @ $5.30

6. What price would one pay to initiate the long 90/95/100 put butterfly position?

7. What are the break-even points?

8. What is the maximum potential profit, and what is the maximum potential loss?

9. What does the P&L diagram look like?

10. What is the profit or loss of the 90/95/100 put butterfly with XYZ stock at the following prices at expiration?

    a. 85
    b. 97
    c. 102

11. If you are short the XYZ 50 call, your position has positive theta. True or false?

12. What is the cost of carry for a 10-point box spread with interest rates at 7 percent and twenty days until expiration?

13. If you were going to buy a box spread, would you buy or sell the in-the-money options?

14. How many "reaction lows" near the same price does it take to form a support level?

15. A trader decides to put on the 40/45 bull put spread. After a market rally, new resistance levels occur and now the trader thinks the market may go sideways for some time and therefore wants to modify his strategy. He could add the 45/50 bear call spread in order to convert the position into an iron butterfly. True or false?

16. Consider the scenario in question 15. If the trader becomes bullish again, how could he convert it back to a bull spread?

17. If you were long the 20/25/30/35 put condor, and the underlying is trading at 26, the outside strikes would have positive thetas. True or false?

18. If the XYZ 80 call has a vega of 0.50 and a premium of $6.00, and there is an increase in volatility of 2 points, what would the new premium be of the 80 call?

Given the condor position below, answer questions 19 to 23:

Long 1 XYZ 85 put @ $10.50
Short 1 XYZ 90 put @ $15.20
Short 1 XYZ 95 put @ $20.20
Long 1 XYZ 100 put @ $25.50

19. What price would one pay to initiate the long 85/90/95/100 put condor position?

20. What are the break-even points?

21. What is the maximum potential profit, and what is the maximum potential loss?

22. What does the P&L diagram look like?

23. What is the profit or loss of the 85/90/95/100 put condor position with XYZ stock at the following prices at expiration?
    a. 92
    b. 99
    c. 103

24. At-the-money options and out-of-the-money options are composed entirely of intrinsic value. True or false?

25. If the delta of the long XYZ 80 call changes from 0.80 to 0.90 with a 1-point change in the underlying price, what would the gamma be?

26. The long broken-wing put butterfly has its embedded credit spread above or below the body?

27. If one sold the 70/80/90 call butterfly and then bought the 70/80 box, what would be the resulting position?

28. A trader has on the long 40/45/50 iron butterfly position. After a period of consolidation, the trader becomes bearish. What could be done to convert the strategy to a bearish position?

29. A 70/75/80 short call butterfly is the combination of a vertical bull spread and a vertical bear spread. True or false?

For questions 30 and 31, use the following information:

The underlying is trading at 97.50.

Calls	*K*	*Puts*
9.50	*90*	*0.63*
5.75	*95*	*1.88*
3.13	*100*	*4.00*

30. Construct the long iron butterfly.

31. What is the amount of debit incurred or credit received for this position?

32. Long 10 May 300/310 call verticals at $7.00 and short 10 May 320/330 call verticals at $3.50. What is this position?

33. A trader puts on a 40/45 bear call spread, and then the underlying drops to a strong support level. The trader feels that the market may begin to move sideways now for a while. What can be added to the existing bear call spread to turn the position into a long iron condor?

34. Suppose the trader in question 33 would now like to convert the position back to a bear spread. What would he need to do?

35. A trader has put on the 20/25 bull put spread. Now he predicts that the underlying will begin trading within a range. What would need to be done in order to convert the 20/25 bull put spread into an iron condor?

Refer to the long Feb 100/110/115 broken-wing put butterfly below for questions 36, 37, and 38.

Buy 1 Feb 100 put @ $0.75
Sell 2 Feb 110 puts @ $4.00
Buy 1 Feb 115 put @ $8.00

36. At expiration, with the option's underlying security at 100, calculate the potential profit/loss of the 100/110/115 broken-wing put butterfly.

37. At expiration, with the option's underlying security at 111, calculate the potential profit/loss of the 100/110/115 broken-wing put butterfly.

38. One can purchase the Feb 100/110/115 broken-wing put butterfly for how much?

39. If a trader closes the short straddle component of a long iron butterfly, with what strategy is he left?

40. An iron condor can be viewed as one bull spread and one bear spread. True or false?

41. The iron butterfly has a long strangle and a __________ __________ embedded in its structure.

42. A long call butterfly (at K_1, K_2, K_3) and a short call spread (at K_3, K_4) also can be viewed as a ______________ spread.

43. A pterodactyl consists of a bull spread at the lower strikes and a bear spread at the upper strikes. True or false?

44. The broken-wing butterfly (condor) is a limited risk/reward structure. True or false?

45. A broken-wing butterfly can be viewed as two positions: a butterfly and a ______________.

46. What strategy might a trader employ if he desires a large area or range of potential maximum profit (and is willing to accept the risk of losing a greater debit)?

47. The maximum loss for a long call or put pterodactyl is the debit incurred to initiate the spread. True or false?

48. With a short iron butterfly, time decay has a negative effect because the trader is hoping for considerable movement in the underlying's price. True or false?

49. With the option's underlying trading at 110 and four days to expiration, which butterfly will have the greatest delta?
    a. 100/110/120
    b. 110/120/130
    c. 90/100/110

50. For the long call butterfly, theta is most harmful at the middle strike. True or false?

Examine the following chart and use it to answer questions 51 through 60:

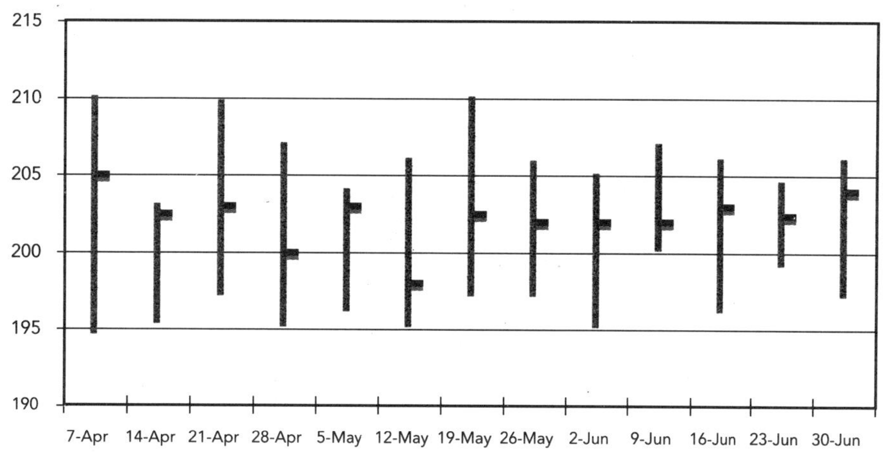

Figure A.1 Trading Range *Source: Corona Derivatives, LLC*

51. At what price level does there appear to be resistance?

52. At what price level does there appear to be support?

53. What area or price appears to be the middle of the range?

54. If you wanted to take advantage of the fact that this underlying looks to be going sideways, what trade could you make?

55. Suppose you wanted to buy a condor. At what strike prices should you place your short options?

56. If you bought the 195/200/205/210 call condor, what would be your area of maximum profitability at expiration?

57. You are long the same condor as in question 56 above. The underlying is currently trading at 202.50. Is your theta positive or negative?

58. You are long the same condor as in questions 56 and 57. The underlying is currently trading at 210. Is your delta positive or negative?

59. Suppose you are long a condor, and suddenly you believe the underlying might break out to the upside. Without liquidating the position entirely, how might you modify your position to take advantage of the breakout?

60. If you bought the 195/200/205 call butterfly and then bought the 200/205/210 call butterfly, what would your position be?

61. You have been bearish on a stock, and your position currently consists of a long put spread. The stock has come down to an important support level and looks like it might start trading sideways for a while. Given you already have an open position, what modification might you make to take advantage of this?

62. If your answer to question 61 above was to buy a call vertical, what is the name of your new position?

63. If your answer to question 61 above was to sell a put vertical, what is the name of your new position?

64. If you buy an ATM butterfly (call or put), and implied volatility rises while all other market factors remain unchanged, what should theoretically happen to the value of your butterfly?

65. If you leg into the ABC 90/95/100 put butterfly for a 0.25 credit, what is the most you could make on the trade?

66. In question 65 above, what is the most you could lose on the trade?

67. In question 65 above, what is the point of maximum profitability?

68. Suppose you buy the 80/85/95 broken-wing call butterfly for 0.50. Where are your break-even points?

69. In question 68 above, what is your maximum possible loss?

70. In question 68 above, what is your maximum possible gain?

Examine the chart below and use it to answer questions 71 to 74:

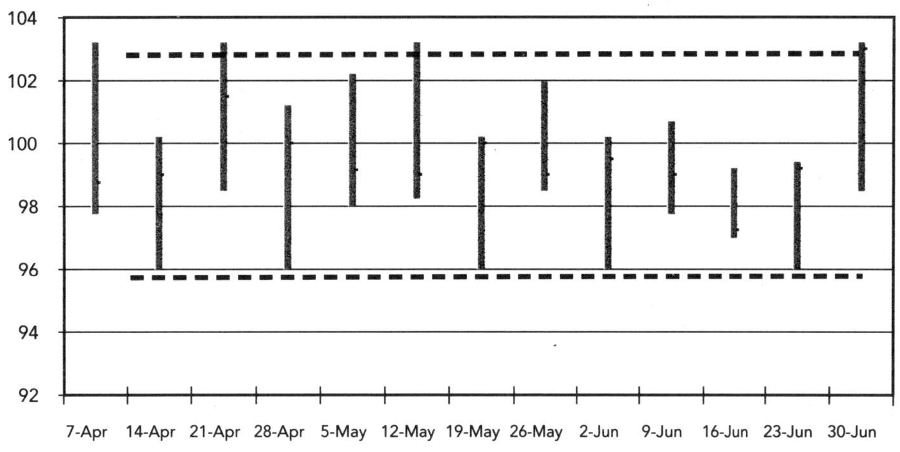

Figure A.2 XYZ Weekly Chart *Source: Corona Derivatives, LLC*

71. At what price level is support?

72. At what price level is resistance?

73. Suppose you decided to put on a long pterodactyl. Which would be better: a call pterodactyl, a put pterodactyl, or an iron pterodactyl?

74. If you decided to buy a long call pterodactyl, which strikes should you buy, which strikes should you sell, and in what amounts?

Supposing you executed the following trade, answer questions 75 to 85:

Buy one XYZ April 96 call at $6.50
Sell one XYZ April 98 call at $5.00
Sell one XYZ April 102 call at $1.50
Buy one XYZ April 104 call at $0.50

75. What trade have you executed?

76. At what price?

77. What is the maximum risk in this position?

78. What is the maximum possible profit?

79. In what price range does the maximum profit occur?

80. If the underlying is sitting at 100.00, do you have a positive or negative theta?

81. If the underlying is sitting at 100.00, do you have positive or negative vega?

82. What is the profit (or loss) of the position if the underlying settles at 104.00 on expiration?

83. What is the profit or loss of the position if the underlying settles at 98.00 at expiration?

84. If the underlying is at 100.00 and implied volatility begins to rise, will the theoretical value of the spread rise or fall?

85. If the underlying is at 96.00 and implied volatility begins to rise, will the theoretical value of the spread rise or fall?

Supposing you executed the following trade, answer questions 86 to 92:

Buy one XYZ April 95 put at $0.50
Sell one XYZ April 105 put at $2.00
Sell one XYZ April 110 put at $5.00
Buy one XYZ April 115 put at $8.00

86. What trade have you executed and for what price?

87. What is your maximum upside risk?

88. What is your maximum downside risk?

89. What is the maximum profit potential?

90. In what price range does the maximum profit occur?

91. Why is the downside risk different from the upside risk?

92. If you bought the April 95/100 put vertical (bought the 100 puts and sold the 95 puts), what would your new position be?

Supposing you executed the following trade, answer questions 93 to 97:

Sell 1 ABC October 55 straddle at $6.50
Buy 1 ABC October 50/60 strangle at $2.00

93. What trade have you executed and for what price?

94. What is the maximum risk in the position?

95. What is the maximum possible profit?

96. At what price does the maximum profit occur?

97. If the underlying hovers around 55.00, is that to the benefit or detriment of this position?

98. If interest rates are zero, what is the equivalent price of the long call butterfly?

99. If interest rates are zero, what is the equivalent price of the long put butterfly?

100. What can cause a difference between the values of a call butterfly and a put butterfly?

Answer Key

1. True
2. True
3. Positive
4. At-the-money
5. Underlying price, interest rates, dividends, time until expiration, implied volatility
6. \$1.15 (–\$1.45 + \$5.60 – \$5.30)
7. \$91.15 (K_1 + debit); \$98.85 (K_3 – debit)
8. \$3.85 ($K_3 - K_1$)/2 – debit; \$1.15 (debit incurred to initiate spread)
9.

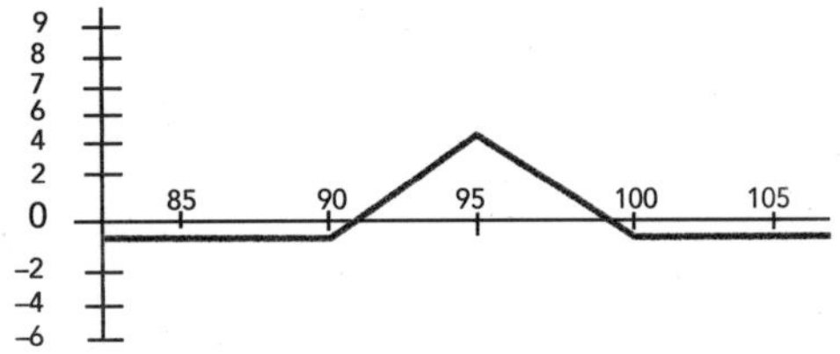

10. a. The 90 put is worth \$5.00, the 95 puts are worth \$10.00 each, and the 100 put is worth \$15.00. Therefore, at expiration it would result in a loss of \$1.15 (+\$5.00 – \$20.00 + 15.00 – \$1.15).
    b. The 90 put is worth \$0.00, the 95 puts are worth \$0.00, and the 100 put is worth \$3.00. Therefore, at expiration it would result in a profit of \$1.85 (+\$0.00 + \$0.00 + \$3.00 – \$1.15).
    c. The 90 put is worth \$0.00, the 95 puts are worth \$0.00, and the 100 put is worth \$0.00. Therefore, at expiration it would result in a loss of \$1.15 (amount paid to initiate the spread).
11. True
12. 0.038 (10 × 0.07 × 20/360)
13. Buy
14. At least two; the more reaction lows in the same area the stronger the support level.
15. True
16. Close out the 45/50 bear call spread
17. False. The outside strikes would have negative thetas.
18. \$7.00 (0.5 vega × 2.00 volatility increase = 1.00 premium increase. 1.00 increase + 6.00 premium = 7.00)
19. \$0.60 (–\$10.50 + \$15.20 + \$20.20 – \$25.50)
20. \$85.60 (K_1 + debit); \$99.40 (K_4 – debit)
21. \$4.40 ($K_3 - K_2$) – debit; \$0.60
22.

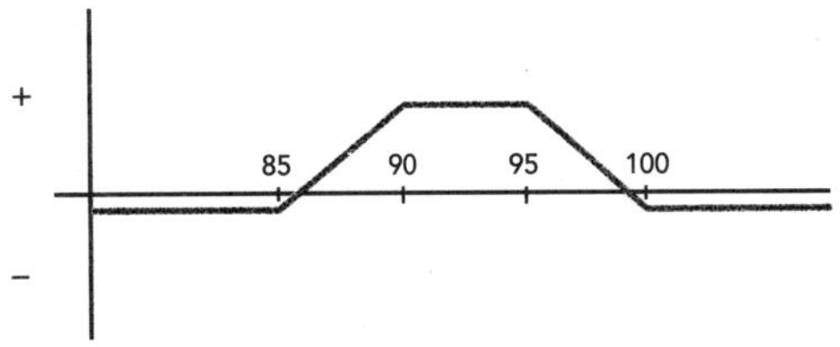

23. a. The 85 put is worth \$0.00, the 90 put is worth \$0.00, the 95 put is worth \$3.00, and the 100 put is worth \$8.00. Therefore, at expiration it would result in a profit of \$4.40 (+\$0.00 – \$0.00 – \$3.00 + \$8.00 – \$0.60).

b. The 85 put is worth $0.00, the 90 put is worth $0.00, the 95 put is worth $0.00, and the 100 put is worth $1.00. Therefore, at expiration it would result in a profit of $0.40 (+$0.00 – $0.00 – $0.00 + $1.00 – $0.60).

c. The 85 put is worth $0.00, the 90 put is worth $0.00, the 95 put is worth $0.00, and the 100 put is worth $0.00. Therefore, at expiration it would result in a loss of $0.60. (+$0.00 – $0.00 – $0.00 + $0.00 – $0.60).

24. False. At-the-money and out-of-the-money options are composed of extrinsic value.
25. 0.10
26. Below
27. Short the 70/80/90 iron butterfly
28. Close out the 40/45 bull put spread
29. True
30. Short the 95 call and 95 put, long the 100 call, long the 90 put
31. $3.87 credit (sold the straddle for $7.63 and purchased the strangle for $3.76)
32. Long call condor
33. Put on a 30/35 bull put vertical spread
34. Close out the bull put vertical spread
35. Put on a 30/35 bear call spread
36. Loss of $5.75:

Long 1 100 put	=	$0.00
Short 2 110 puts	=	–$20.00
Long 1 115 put	=	$15.00
Net value of spread	=	–$5.00
Cost of spread	=	$0.75
Net profit/loss	**=**	**–$5.75**

37. Profit of $3.25:

Long 1 100 put	=	$0.00
Short 2 110 puts	=	$0.00
Long 1 115 put	=	$4.00
Net value of spread	=	$4.00
Cost of spread	=	$0.75
Net profit/loss	**=**	**$3.25**

38. Debit of $0.75
39. Long strangle
40. True
41. Short straddle
42. Broken-wing call butterfly at K_1, K_2, K_4.
43. True
44. True
45. Vertical spread (credit spread)
46. Pterodactyl
47. True
48. True
49. a. 100/110/120
50. False. Theta is most helpful at the middle strike, where the position is profitable.
51. 210.00

52. 195.00
53. Between 200.00 and 205.00; or 202.50
54. Long Condor
55. 200.00, 205.00
56. Between 200.00 and 205.00
57. Positive
58. Negative
59. Buy back the bear spread component.
60. Long 195/200/205/210 call condor
61. Sell a put spread/buy a call spread and create a long butterfly or condor.
62. Long "guts" iron butterfly or condor
63. Long put butterfly or condor
64. It should fall.
65. 05.25
66. You could not lose.
67. 95.00
68. 80.50, 89.50
69. 05.50
70. 04.50
71. 95
72. 103
73. There would be no difference.
74. Buy 1 96, sell 1 98, sell 1 102, buy 1 104.
75. Long call pterodactyl
76. 0.50 debit
77. 0.50
78. 1.50
79. 98.00 to 102.00
80. Positive
81. Negative
82. 0.50 loss
83. 1.50 profit
84. It will fall.
85. It will rise.
86. Buy the long 95/105/110/115 broken-wing put condor at 1.50.
87. 1.50
88. 6.50
89. 3.50
90. Between 105.00 and 110.00
91. Because of the asymmetrical structure (or the embedded short 95/100 put spread)
92. Long the 100/105/110/115 put condor
93. Buy the ABC October 50/55/60 iron butterfly at 4.50 credit.
94. 0.50
95. 4.50
96. 55.00
97. Benefit
98. 0.50
99. 0.50
100. Possible early exercise situation involving American-style options.

Appendix B

GLOSSARY

American-style options: An option contract that can be exercised on or before the expiration date.

at-the-money (ATM): An option contract that has an exercise (strike) price that is equal to the current market price of the underlying security.

away-from-the-money: An option contract that is either in-the-money or out-of-the-money.

bear vertical spread: A vertical spread with a bearish bias, where one purchases a higher strike option and sells a lower strike option of the same class and expiration. Usually, a bear spread using calls (also known as a *short call spread*) will result in an initial credit and a bear spread using puts (also known as a *long put spread*) will result in an initial debit.

body: The inner strike(s) of a butterfly or condor structure.

box spread: An option spread that involves a long call and a short put at one strike price and a short call and long put at another strike price, all in the same expiration month.

broken-wing butterfly: Similar in structure to a standard butterfly; however, the wings (outer strikes) are not equidistant from the body (middle strike).

bull vertical spread: A vertical spread with a bullish bias, where one purchases a lower strike option and sells a higher strike option of the same class and expiration. Usually a bull spread using calls (also known as a *long call spread*) will result in an initial debit and a bull spread using puts (also known as a *short put spread*) will result in an initial credit.

butterfly: A spread that consists of three (usually) adjacent strikes of the same option type with the same expiration on the same underlying security. The strategy usually has both limited risk and limited profit potential. A long butterfly position is constructed by purchasing the lowest strike option, selling two middle strike options, and purchasing the higher strike option.

calendar spread: A spread that consists of the simultaneous purchase and sale of options of the same class, type, and strike price, but with different expiration dates

call: A contract between a buyer and a seller where the buyer has the right, but not the obligation, to purchase an underlying security at a specific price (exercise or strike price), on or before a specific date (expiration date). The seller of a call option assumes the obligation of delivering (at the specific exercise price) the underlying security should a buyer of the call option choose to exercise the right to purchase.

carrying cost: The amount of interest expense on money borrowed to finance a position.

classic long iron butterfly: This strategy incorporates both calls and puts. It is the combination of a short straddle and a long strangle. The position structure is long a put at a lower strike, short a call and put at the next higher strike, and long a call at the next higher strike. This structure may also be viewed as a bear call spread at the higher strikes overlapping a bull put spread at the lower strikes.

consolidation: A market condition where, after a directional move, the market goes sideways in a "resting" phase.

credit spread: A vertical spread where the option sold has a higher price than the option purchased, resulting in an initial net credit. A call bear spread and a put bull spread are examples of credit spreads.

debit spread: A vertical spread where the option purchased has a higher price than the option sold, resulting in an initial net debit. A call bull spread and a put bear spread are examples of debit spreads.

delta: The sensitivity (rate of change) of an option's theoretical value (assessed value) to a $1 move of the underlying instrument. Delta is the probability that the option will expire in-the-money.

early exercise situation: A situation where, usually due to cost of carry or dividend considerations, it may be beneficial to the owner of an American-style put or call to exercise the option prior to expiration.

European-style option: An option contract that can be exercised only at expiration.

extrinsic value: The portion of an option price that cannot be attributed to intrinsic value.

gamma: The sensitivity (rate of change) of an option's delta with respect to a 1-point change in the underlying instrument. It may be viewed as the quantity of underlying produced in a $1 move of the underlying.

guts: Guts are similar to strangles in that they consist of the purchase (or sale) of both a put and a call at different strikes on the same underlying security with the same expiration. However, unlike the strangle, the guts consists of both a lower strike call and a higher strike put. The guts will therefore have some intrinsic value at expiration, whereas the strangle could potentially finish worthless. The guts' value at expiration comes from either the call or the put finishing in-the-money, or a combination of both the call and put finishing in-the-money.

historical volatility: A measure of the actual price fluctuations of an underlying instrument over a given period of time.

hockey-stick graphs: Graphs showing the outcome of an option strategy at various underlying prices, at expiration.

implied volatility: The determination of the volatility component of an option theoretical pricing model by using current prices along with other known variables. It may be viewed as the market's forecast as to what the average volatility of the underlying might be during the remaining time to expiration.

in-the-money (ITM): An option that has intrinsic value. A call option is in-the-money if the strike price is below the underlying security's current market price. A put option is in-the-money if the strike price is above the underlying security's current market price.

intrinsic value: The amount by which an option is in-the-money.

iron pterodactyl: An iron pterodactyl is a regular pterodactyl with a synthetically equivalent credit spread substituted for the debit spread portion of the position.

long: Owning or having bought an asset.

long call spread: A long call spread consists of buying the lower strike call and selling the higher strike call.

long condor: A condor incorporates four strikes of the same class and type having the same expirations. It is constructed by purchasing one option at the lowest strike, selling an option at the next two higher strikes, and purchasing one option at the highest strike.

long put spread: A long put spread consists of buying the higher strike put and selling the lower strike put.

moneyness: The location of an option strike relative to the underlying security's price. See **in-the-money**, **at-the-money**, **out-of-the-money**, and **away-from-the money**.

out-of-the-money (OTM): An option contract that has no intrinsic value. A call option is out-of-the-money if the exercise price is higher than the underlying security's current market price. A put option is out-of-the-money if the exercise price is below the underlying security's current market price.

P&L: Industry abbreviation for "profit and loss."

pterodactyl: The pterodactyl is a long condor with a gap between the middle strikes. It retains the bull spread at the lower strikes, bear spread at the upper strikes composition. The distance between the wing strikes and the body strikes are equal, giving it a symmetrical P&L diagram.

put: A contract between a buyer and a seller where the buyer has the right, but not the obligation, to sell an underlying security at a specific price (exercise or strike price), on or before a specific date (exercise date). The seller of a put option assumes the obligation of receiving (at the specific exercise price) the underlying security should a buyer of the put option choose to exercise the right to sell.

resistance level: A price level or zone located above the current market price where sellers become more willing to sell and buyers are reluctant to buy.

scalp: To quickly buy and sell a futures contract for a small profit.

scalper: A speculator who buys and sells often to take advantage of small price fluctuations. The scalper tries to make many small profits on large turnover by positioning himself with the order flow. This type of trading can add a great deal of liquidity to the market.

short: Having sold an asset not previously owned and being obligated to repurchase it at some time in the future.

short call spread: A short call spread consists of selling the lower strike call and purchasing the higher strike call.

short put spread: A short put spread consists of selling the higher strike put and purchasing the lower strike put.

straddle: A spread involving the purchase (or sale) of an equal number of both puts and calls with the same underlying instrument, strike price, and expiration.

strangle: A spread that involves the purchase (or sale) of an equal number of puts and calls with the same underlying and expiration, but with different strikes. These strikes are out-of-the-money (unlike the guts) and are usually, but not always, bracketing the current price of the underlying.

support level: A range or zone located below the current market price where buyers become more willing to buy and sellers are reluctant to sell.

synthetic: Two or more trading vehicles (call, put, underlying) packaged together to emulate another trading vehicle or spread. Some examples include:

(long call = long put + long underlying) (short call = short put + short underlying)

(long put = long call + short underlying) (short put = short call + long underlying)

(long underlying = long call + short put) (short underlying = short call + long put)

theta: The sensitivity (rate of change) of theoretical option prices with regard to small changes in time. Theta measures the rate of decay in the time value of options. Theta may be expressed as the amount of erosion of an option's theoretical value over one day in time.

trading range market: When the forces of supply and demand equalize, a stalemate occurs and the market moves sideways between support and resistance levels.

vega: The sensitivity (rate of change) of an option's theoretical value to a change in implied volatility. Vega may be expressed as the number of points of theoretical value gained or lost from a 1 percent rise or fall in implied volatility.

vertical spread: The simultaneous purchase and sale of options with the same class and expiration but with different strike prices. Depending on which strike is bought and which strike is sold, they can have either a bullish or bearish bias. For example: XYZ July 100/105 call vertical spread. If the trader were bullish, he would buy the 100 call and sell the 105 call; if bearish, he would buy the 105 call and sell the 100 call.

wings: The outer strikes of a butterfly or condor structure.

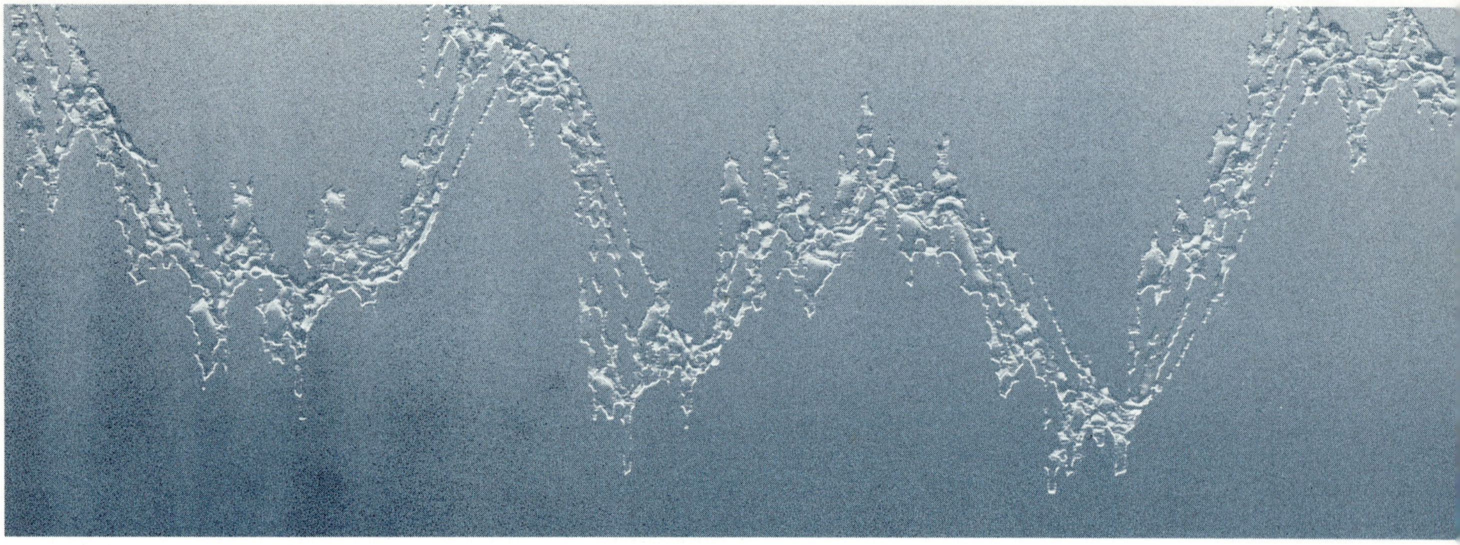

Index

V

W

About the Authors

Anthony J. Saliba has been a pioneer and active participant in the derivatives markets for more than twenty-five years. Derivatives activities have spanned derivatives trading, training, and developing electronic trading systems and solutions. He began his career trading equity options as an independent market maker at the Chicago Board Options Exchange (CBOE) in 1979. Over the next decade, he gained extensive experience in trading currencies, equities, and S&P 500 and S&P 100 contracts. In each of these markets, he emerged as a dominant and respected presence and quickly acquired a reputation as one of the top traders. His trading accomplishments, most notably his success during the crash of '87, earned him a place in the national bestseller *Market Wizards: Interviews with Top Traders*, by Jack Schwager.

Due to his innovative trading ideas, Saliba has become an internationally recognized consultant on the emergence and function of electronic markets and trading systems. He is often quoted in industry publications, including the *Wall Street Journal*, the *Financial Times*, and www.theStreet.com, and is frequently invited to speak at industry forums. He has founded numerous industry-related companies, including Saliba Partners, LLC (1984–1999), a proprietary options trading firm that included a Designated Primary Market Maker (DPM) floor operation on the Chicago Board Options Exchange; International Trading Institute, Ltd. (1989), a derivatives consulting and training firm providing advanced options trading education to large institutional market participants; First Traders Analytical Solutions, LLC (1992), a provider of front- and middle-office trading, pricing, and risk-management systems; LiquidPoint, LLC (1999), a broker-dealer offering options execution/facilitation and enhanced liquidity and potential price improvement for many large Wall Street firms; and Saliba Portfolio Management, LLC (2002), a portfolio management firm providing state-of-the-art investment enhancement techniques through the use of derivatives. In July 2007, Saliba's firm, LiquidPoint, LLC, became part of BNY ConvergEx Group, a leading global agency brokerage and investment technology firm. Saliba is a director of BNY ConvergEx Group and continues to serve as president and CEO of LiquidPoint.

Joseph C. Corona has been actively involved in trading options for more than twenty-five years. During this time he traded on the floors of the Chicago Board Options Exchange, the Chicago Board of Trade, the

Chicago Mercantile Exchange, and the London International Financial Futures and Options Exchange, as well as in the over-the-counter markets and the major electronic venues. During the course of his career he has traded equity, equity index, fixed income, currency, energy, and commodities options both as a market maker and proprietary trader. In addition, he has extensive experience in the training and management of derivatives traders and has built and managed trading desks in the United States, Europe, and Asia.

Corona has also been an adjunct instructor at International Trading Institute since 1990, delivering courses in advanced options trading and risk analysis techniques to hundreds of traders and trading desks in North, South, and Central America; Europe; and Asia. He also contributes to various financial markets websites and is a frequent speaker at industry conferences.

Karen E. Johnson joined Saliba in 1992 and has been actively involved in the start-up and/or management of a number of Saliba-affiliated companies, including Saliba Partners, First Traders Analytical Solutions, LiquidPoint, SalibaCo, LLC, International Trading Institute, and Saliba Portfolio Management. Her focus has been in the areas of business and product development, operations management, and sales. Presently, she is COO of Saliba Portfolio Management.

Johnson is the former president of International Trading Institute and currently serves on its board of directors. Throughout her fifteen years with the Saliba companies, she has spent much of her time working with global financial institutions developing curricula and training programs for both established markets and such emerging marketplaces as Mexico, Panama, Colombia, Korea, Malaysia, and Poland.

Her previous publishing experience includes developing the concept and managing the writing and publication of *The Options Workbook: Fundamental Spread Concepts and Strategies*, by Anthony J. Saliba and the staff of International Trading Institute. Currently in its third edition, it has proven to be an excellent educational tool for the novice investor or trader.

About International Trading Institute

Anthony J. Saliba's awareness of the need for derivatives education in the marketplace inspired him to start International Trading Institute (ITI) in 1989. ITI offers hands-on options trading workshops delivered by professional traders. The hallmark of the ITI curriculum is the fostering of rigor and discipline in trading and risk management. ITI is an internationally renowned firm that has trained more than five thousand students from over thirty countries in the past eighteen years. Clientele include many large global financial institutions such as Citibank, DeutscheBank, UBS, and Credit Suisse. We invite you to visit our website, www.itichicago.com, for more information about our workshops or for additional option strategy lessons and commentary.